Conten

Foreword

By the Reverend Frank Drake, M.A., Oxon, formerly Principal of Bishop Cotton School, Simla, Warden of the Chapel of Christ the Healer, Guernsey, and author of *Thy Son Liveth*.

About this book

Carolyn is calling it *Love, The Eternal Link*. But what is it, this link? Is it not just another name for that essential relationship, forged by our Creator himself, which binds us to Him and to one another, and which, for Christians at least, was historically expressed in the life of Christ, given as a living illustration of the link of love which binds earth to heaven, man to God, present weakness to future strength?

Although, sadly, this link goes so repeatedly unrecognised, overlooked or forgotten, we, each of us, will one day return to Him, and to heaven. How we are likely to fare when we get there is recorded for us in an early chapter of this book through a series of deeply interesting revelations, messages, sent from heaven by one who calls himself the Messenger, about the conditions which he himself has found there.

There are no doubt some Christians, or at least some church-goers, who will claim, concerning these revelations, that the New Testament already tells us all we need to know about the next world. This may have been true until fairly recently, but surely the unprecedented advances in human knowledge in virtually every other subject constitute a challenge to us to explore this last one – that is, the ultimate destination of the human spirit?

LOVE, THE ETERNAL LINK
Evidence of Immortality

Acknowledgements

First and foremost, I would like to express my gratitude to the Reverend Frank Drake, M.A., Oxon, for all his advice and help with this book. His unfailing interest and deep understanding have been a source of immense encouragement to me, and I much appreciate his kindness in writing the Foreword and the final chapter, 'Shafts of Light'.

I would also specially like to thank the family of the late Mrs Elizabeth Bedford for their support, she having given me permission to use material from her husband Stanley Bedford's three books, *Death An Interesting Journey*, *The Mysteries of Life* and *Life Here and Hereafter*; also from Mr Roger Walker's book, *To Faith Add Knowledge*.

I am greatly indebted to all the kind friends and acquaintances who have supplied me with accounts of their experiences beyond the physical senses, and to Dr G. G. Macdonald, M.D., F.R.C.G.P. and Dr Derek Doyle, M.B., Ch.B., M.R.C.G.P. and other members of the medical profession who wish to remain anonymous.

I gratefully acknowledge permission to quote from *The Swan in the Evening* by Rosamond Lehmann, published by Virago Press Limited, 1982. Copyright © Rosamond Lehmann 1967. (First published by William Collins Limited, 1967.)

My final thanks go to my husband and family, whose help, patience and co-operation have been invaluable.

LOVE, THE ETERNAL LINK
Evidence of Immortality

by

Carolyn de la Hey

A companion volume to *Lifeline* by the same author

William Sessions Limited
The Ebor Press, York, England

First Published in 1988

Reprinted 1990

ISBN 1 85072 038 X

By the same author
Lifeline
(Published by Neville Spearman (Jersey) Limited in 1978)

Printed in 12/13 Plantin Typeface
by William Sessions Limited
The Ebor Press, York, England

There are some who believe that the veil between this world and the next is rapidly becoming thinner, so that the last unexplored frontier might seem about to open before our eyes.

It should be remembered that the teachings of Jesus, limited, so far as we know, to three short years, and recorded only as a series of short sentences which takes just a little time to read but a lifetime to digest fully, concentrated mainly upon the importance of right living in this world and said little about the next. Jesus Himself admitted, very shortly before His death, that His teaching was incomplete. In St John's Gospel (*New English Bible*, John, 16.12) we read, 'There is still much that I could say to you, but the burden would be too great for you now.' That was 2,000 years ago! Earlier He had said 'Seek, and ye shall find . . .'

For myself, I cannot find that the teachings of the Messenger in any way run counter to the teachings of Jesus, his Master and mine. They interpret and expand them, and will, I am sure, bring comfort to those who seek enlightenment and consolation.

So far as the link of love is concerned, the Messenger tells us that 'Love is the strongest link [sic] between heaven and earth, and the more you learn to love while you are on earth, the better you will harmonise with your surroundings when you come to heaven.' And if any should be surprised that I, as a Christian priest, should be prepared to accept the validity of such messages, I can only reply, 'How could I refuse to do so? For I, like many other priests, have on occasion received such messages myself, unsought and unexpected, which altered my patterns of thought and fundamentally changed the direction of my life.' Some of these are recorded in Chapter VI.

About the authoress

I am honoured and delighted by Carolyn de la Hey's invitation to write a foreword, and to add an appendix to this, her second book, for I have long held her in great affection and esteem.

Carolyn possesses a deep, natural and spontaneous religious sense which governs all her personal philosophy and thinking, but never expresses itself in any form of bigotry. Though a convinced

Christian, she does not consider herself bound by loyalty to any one denomination or church. Possessed also, from childhood, of a strong psychic awareness and a keen interest in psychic experience, she has never herself become a spiritualist.

In short, I have always found in her an admirable and easy tolerance of other people and their opinions.

Well read in philosophy and religious works, she has lived and travelled widely in European countries, has worked in London in a number of interesting jobs, including a spell in the Press Office of the Dorchester Hotel, was for many years a keen skier and is now a keen golfer. She is married, with two daughters and lives in the Channel Island of Jersey.

Her great personal charm and gift of easy companionship are perhaps best illustrated by the fact that as a younger woman she was offered, but for various reasons was unable to accept, the post of lady-in-waiting to the wife of a Governor-General of New Zealand. In short she has so far led a colourful and varied life which cannot fail to have contributed to her understanding and experience.

I know that her only purpose in writing both this book, and her former book *Lifeline*, has been to share with others the joyful truths which she has discovered for herself.

Introduction

As we grow older and perhaps have to face difficulties and bereavements, many questions about the purpose of life and survival of death arise in our minds. We also want to know whether the link of love between ourselves and those from whom we are apparently separated by physical death, is an eternal one, extending beyond the grave.

It was the realisation that I myself possessed some psychic and spiritual faculty which led to my interest in these matters, in the unseen and in other people's perception beyond the senses. I have been able over the years to assemble certain vital revelations from the spirit world together with accounts from reliable people of their own psychic and spiritual experiences, all of which, directly or indirectly, indicate the permanent nature of the link of love. Some of these are recorded in this book, in the hope that they may be a source of interest and encouragement.

I am well aware that within the Christian church there are those who oppose any attempts to investigate life beyond the present, and that there are passages in the Old Testament expressly denouncing all forms of investigation into the afterlife. However, Christians live by the more advanced guidance given in the New Testament. Christ preached 'forgive thine enemies' in contrast to the primitive Old Testament practice of taking revenge by exacting an 'eye for an eye'. St Paul accepts the reality of spiritual forces and in his first epistle to the Corinthians (Cor. 12.7-10) he says, 'But the manifestation of the Spirit is given to every man to profit withal. For to one is given by the Spirit the word of wisdom, to another the word of knowledge by the same Spirit; To another faith by the same Spirit; to another the gifts of healing by the same Spirit; to another the working of miracles; to another prophecy; to another discerning of spirits; . . .'

A genuine spiritual gift can only be beneficial to all concerned. Of course there may be individuals who falsely claim to possess one or more of these powers and one should be aware of this possibility.

Let me now introduce two leading characters in the book. About four centuries ago there lived in England a man named Thomas Owen whose great intelligence, unquestioned integrity and unstinted service to his country earned him a place in Westminster Abbey, where his tomb still stands in the south aisle.

In 1938 a remarkable Welsh woman named Elizabeth Bedford discovered that she was becoming a trance medium. In spite of her dismayed resistance (for at that time she deeply disapproved of anything in the nature of spiritualism) she repeatedly experienced states of unconsciousness akin to deep sleep, and during these periods messages, spoken aloud through her unconscious mediumship, were given by a man now living, as he claimed, in heaven. He gave her his name, during earth life, as having been Thomas Owen, and in support of this claim gave details of his past life, occupation and dwelling places. These facts were later verified.

During the trances Elizabeth remained totally unaware that any messages were coming through her, but happily they were recorded by her husband Stanley, who was able to ask questions and to receive answers. We owe a great debt to his dedication in this matter.

Yielding at last to her outstanding gift as a trance medium, she joined the College of Psychic Studies in London where, in 1963, I had the privilege of meeting her. I was immediately drawn to her warm personality, her obvious honesty and her quick sense of humour. This meeting was to develop into a close friendship which lasted until her death in 1979.

Thomas Owen indicated that he no longer wished to be known by his earth-life name, but as 'The Messenger' by which he clearly meant 'A Messenger from Heaven', or 'Angel', presumably for the following reason: in our New Testament, which was written in Greek, the Greek word for messenger was *angelos*, and early translators of the New Testament very reasonably preferred to translate *angelos*, not as messenger, but as angel. Since therefore he insists that he is now living in heaven, the Messenger must surely intend his messages to be regarded as coming from a lofty source, and himself as being one of our guardian angels, at least in so far as teaching is concerned. What he has to say later in this book, under the heading 'Guardian Angels', would seem to confirm this view.

As human beings we shall always be challenged by mysteries beyond our comprehension. But those of us who have begun to seek will surely recognise the truth of the Messenger's underlying theme, that love is such a strong and eternal link between God and ourselves, and ourselves and one another, that even physical death cannot break it.

****

Some of the contents of this book enlarge upon matters already described briefly in *Lifeline*. I have found it necessary to include such material, particularly in relation to the identity of the Messenger.

CHAPTER I

Early Signposts

MY OWN SEEKING HAS ARISEN out of a gentle progression of intermittent revelations, and psychic and spiritual experiences, which began in my early childhood. These seemingly unconnected events, though I did not realise it at the time, formed a pattern and acted as signposts to help me on my spiritual journey.

Like many others, I have, since my earliest memories, been aware of an invisible reality – helped no doubt by a religious upbringing. At the age of nine I reached my first signpost which awakened in me a strange mystical awareness; an awareness that there existed in me, and also somehow beyond me, a small but exciting area independent of my five senses. My cousin and I were enjoying a vigorous ball game in the sunny garden of my grandmother's cottage in Devon. The front door was open, and suddenly the ball disappeared down the dark hallway. Breathless and laughing I rushed after it, and having retrieved it, paused for a moment. A single streak of sunlight fell upon a tapestry poem hanging on the wall, brilliantly illuminating it as I read: 'I expect to pass through this world but once . . .' Instantly there followed a moment of profound recognition. The idea of the journey, the passing through this world, was immediately familiar to me and I felt within myself the truth of immortality. A banging door broke the spell, abruptly returning me to the present and the urgency of the ball game, but the memory of this compelling episode remains with me to this day.

During my education at a convent school we were given a fair amount of religious instruction, and encouraged to think and act in

1

accordance with Christian beliefs. However, the following experience touched me at a deeper level than that of the intellect. This second signpost showed me the possibility of receiving revelation, and confirmed my belief in immortality.

I was about 14 at the time. The scene was the swimming pool, set in the convent gardens. I was alone, practising enthusiastically for an end of term race. Length after length I covered until eventually, quite exhausted, I heaved myself out of the water and made my way to the dressing room – a small plain hut with no furnishing save a mirror on the wall.

My mind was blank as I took my towel and slowly wiped my eyes, gazing into the glass. Suddenly I saw, as it were, into myself, layer after layer. I looked past my dripping face and body, and past my changing personality, until I reached a glowing spark – my real self – existing permanently. This 'core' did not belong only in time, for through it I felt again my own link with eternity and was deeply shaken. All was silent about me, then a loudly clanging bell summoning us to the classrooms interrupted this beautiful and thought-provoking revelation.

Years passed, enriched by a variety of inner and outer pre-occupations, and then in my early twenties I was given an uplifting new experience. This was the third signpost and revealed that the dead can come into close contact with the living. My grandmother, with whom I had shared a special bond since childhood, had been dead for several months before she made her presence known to me. On two occasions I felt her at my side, instantly recognising her warm and happy personality, and hearing what she was telling me about future happenings. Subsequently these prophecies proved to be true. I felt great joy in her company, and the fact that she was watching over the family and knew of our activities gave me a pleasant feeling of security. Above all I was grateful to God for showing me that the link of love continues after death.

These events stimulated my interest in the unseen, and friends whom I questioned described to me their experiences of perception beyond the senses. By now I was eager to learn more about the spirit world.

Thus it was that I reached my fourth signpost – a highly significant stage in the journey: my meeting with Mrs Elizabeth Bedford in the early 1960s, at the College of Psychic Studies in London.

Mrs Bedford was an engaging personality whom one instinctively trusted. As our friendship developed I learned to appreciate her character as well as her outstanding gift. She was kind and fair to everyone, deeply sympathetic to those in need, and the most generous person I have met. She was also strict, both with herself and with others. At all times mediumship was to be treated with respect and valued as a gift from God. Mrs Bedford was a practical woman, and she organised an immaculate home. 'Put your house in order' was one of her favourite maxims, meaning not just the house but all the commitments of one's life. Another of her favourite sayings was 'Right is Might', and she certainly lived according to her ideals, thus providing an inspiring example for those who knew and loved her.

The Messenger, who spoke through her while she was in trance, gave me the evidence of survival I sought, and much spiritual enlightenment. The opportunity of taking part in these unforgettable talks was a highlight in my life which came precisely at the right time. For I would not have been ready for the knowledge available through Mrs Bedford's mediumship without my own previous signposts, which to me so strongly suggested the existence of the unseen world.

One day Mrs Bedford invited me to their home to meet her husband Stanley. They lived in a neat Victorian house overlooking a park. Their little garden was Stanley's joy, and when he was not writing or busy with other demands he was at his happiest tending the flowers.

Stanley Bedford was a quiet man, with fine features and a gentle manner. He had been involved in music engraving and welfare work before his retirement. Of the two characters he was the thinker, and searcher for truth, and Mrs Bedford told me of the encouragement and support he had given her in her work as a medium.

Stanley died in his eighties, and shortly afterwards Elizabeth left London in order to set up home with her son and daughter-in-law, Mary, in Devon. One sunny June evening we were all standing in the garden admiring the roses, and I felt a deep contentment. Then came the realisation that our companionship could not last. "I know it's selfish" I told Elizabeth, "but how I shall miss you when you go to heaven". "I'll be closer to you when I've gone" was her reassuring reply.

When she became ill she moved into the cottage hospital nearby, and died in her sleep one evening. An extraordinary sense of loss stayed with me for a while, then was gently transformed into gratitude.

Some time after her death, when her daughter-in-law Mary was dying of cancer after a prolonged illness, Elizabeth responded to my appeal for help. This showed me that those whom we have temporarily lost through death can instantly reach us.

I had just heard from her son, who telephoned me after seeing Mary in hospital. "The doctors think that she might live for a fortnight, or maybe only days" he said in great distress. I tried to comfort him, then returned to the kitchen where I was preparing supper. I stood quietly alone, then summoning all my strength, directed my thoughts to Elizabeth. "I'm so upset for the family" I whispered, "and I'm sending you my love and asking for help in these heart-rending circumstances". Much relieved by this prayer, I turned my attention back to the cooking.

I went to bed early, feeling quite relaxed. As I was sitting in the bathroom combing my hair, I felt a sudden lightness of heart regarding Mary. Then I sensed Elizabeth at my right side, and 'heard' her comforting voice saying, "Don't worry, we're moving in now". Mary's voice followed, "It's so easy, Mother's meeting me" she said. A moment afterwards an irresistible force approached me from my left side – like a strong wind, and more uplifting than anything one could imagine. I bowed my head in reverence as this force stamped into my mind the words "Faith means accepting everything".

4

I lost count of time, then suddenly I was back in a normal state of consciousness. I warned my husband that I thought Mary was dying. At eight o'clock the following morning one of Mary's daughters telephoned me in tears. When she said "Mummy died early this morning" my first reaction was one of shock, swiftly followed by a feeling of profound gratitude. For I had been shown dramatically that through the link of love those in the spirit world can respond immediately to our needs, and put clear messages into our minds. This knowledge has had a tremendous effect on my life.

The vivid statement 'Faith means accepting everything' had particular significance for me at that time because it answered my question. I had been wondering sadly why Mary and her husband, who had been so kind to Elizabeth in her old age, were not permitted to enjoy a few years of freedom together. Now, through the power of the spirit, I knew that I must accept God's will in the matter, even when confronted by mysteries beyond my understanding.

Looking back to the beginning of my interest in the sixth sense, I realise that it was after my grandmother's death that my faculty for hearing, and occasionally for seeing, beyond the senses developed quickly without any effort on my part. Such events do not occur frequently in my life, but when they do, I always learn something of importance.

The fifth signpost in my spiritual journey was marked 'Beware', and showed me that in certain circumstances we receive divine protection. One day I was preparing to drive home, having spent a pleasant afternoon with a friend. I noted that I had stayed with her 10 minutes longer than I had intended to, as guests would soon be arriving at our house. However I was not worried – on the contrary, I felt happy and relaxed after the visit – and being familiar with the stretch of road ahead, knew that if I drove quickly I should soon be home.

Then, to my amazement, as I fastened my seat belt I distinctly heard the words "Drive home carefully". This message was accompanied by a sickening feeling of apprehension in the pit of my stomach. I had no choice but to obey.

So I drove slowly along with the utmost care, observing that there was very little traffic about. Then upon turning a corner I saw a car approaching on the other side of the road. Suddenly, to my horror, like a streak of lightning, a red sports car overtook this vehicle at tremendous speed, missing me by inches as I slammed on the brakes and pulled in to the hedge. It was only my slow driving that prevented a nasty accident involving three cars. I have often wondered whose was the voice warning me of the imminent danger, and whether it was my relaxed frame of mind that enabled the warning to penetrate?

When I reached the sixth signpost a sad episode led to my being granted a new vision.

I had a close friend a little older than myself, whom I had known well for many years. Our relationship consisted of deep affection, shared interests and mutual friends, much laughter and some differences of opinion.

Shortly before my friend's sudden death we were all, family and friends, enjoying ourselves and making plans for future celebrations. It was a particularly happy time.

Then came her totally unexpected illness which increased rapidly in severity and resulted in her being admitted to hospital. She was too ill for any visitors save those of the immediate family. A large bunch of her favourite flowers with a short message was my only possible contribution. No time for goodbyes. A few days later she died peacefully in her sleep, leaving us all stunned by the shock, and grief-stricken.

A few nights after her death, I lay in bed and talked to her of all my feelings. I said "I'm glad that you were spared further suffering, but you are much missed on earth. Now you are somewhere higher, in the hands of our Creator. I shall raise my thoughts as I try to reach you, putting aside events in our shared time in this world, and concentrating upon you with all my love and gratitude."

Suddenly it was as if I was plucked from my body and lifted up into a world of quiet perfection; a distant place too beautiful to describe. While I was still enjoying the beauty and embrace of this wondrous new world, my friend came to join me; at once I recognised her personality and her voice. *"Peace,* darling", she said. Then, just as suddenly, I was back again in my body, lying comfortably in bed.

I well understand the reason for the briefness of my vision. No-one entering and remaining in that wonderful place could bear to leave it. How I value that uplifting contact, and that glimpse of the perfection to come, which so tranquilly eased the pain of parting.

The seventh and final signpost at this stage of my journey was discovered at a very difficult time.

I was feeling low, both mentally and physically; trying to do my best but lacking the enthusiasm and energy. In short, I felt that there were more demands upon me than I could cope with. So, in desperation one night, I turned to God and prayed from the depth of my heart "Please help me – I can't continue like this." I repeated the prayer several times before falling asleep.

Suddenly in the middle of the night I awoke – intensely happy, wrapped in a warm 'cocoon' of pure spiritual love. I was sustained by love and fully aware of my beautiful state, and knew that just as I myself was loved and precious, so each individual is loved and precious. Then, as my 'cocoon' gently faded, the knowledge came to me that I would be given all the strength I needed.

So moving was this event that upon returning to my normal state of consciousness I found that tears of emotion and happiness were running down my cheeks, and in the darkness I whispered over and over again "I want God . . . I want God".

The following morning I re-lived the experience with wonder and with gratitude. The much needed strength was there for me, and has remained so.

Inevitably, I began to realise more and more the need for self-purification, and as the years passed received moments of guidance in this task. The first of these occurred after I had offered up a prayer one night just before falling asleep. I prayed "Lord, I know that my first step in attempting to reach you must be to purify myself", and then listed several of my known shortcomings,

7

including worry. The next morning, in a half-waking state, I understood that I was being taught something, by being lifted to a higher and more generous level of thinking. I became extremely happy, filled with joy, and approached the new day with a loving concern for other people. I had no worries about myself, only this strong desire to care for others. Gradually, I dropped back into my normal consciousness, and set about preparing breakfast. But the lesson was firmly embedded in my mind. 'Purify yourself in order to love better.' It was then that I began to understand and to accept the tremendous importance of Our Lord's command 'Love one another'.

Having related these few experiences of my own, I hope that I may have indicated the possibilities of psychic and spiritual contact which are available to so many of us. Let us next, however, consider the fascinating work of my friend Elizabeth Bedford, together with the efforts made by herself and her husband Stanley, to identify the Messenger.

CHAPTER II

The Messenger's Identity

The following two chapters are based on the teachings recorded in Stanley Bedford's three illuminating books: 'Death – An Interesting Journey', 'The Mysteries of Life', 'Life Here and Hereafter' and Roger Walker's book 'To Faith Add Knowledge'.

WRITING ABOUT ELIZABETH, Stanley Bedford has recorded: 'My wife was a most reluctant medium. She had never read a book on the subject. Prior to the discovery of her amazing gift, and for some time afterwards, she was, in accordance with her religious upbringing, distinctly opposed to spiritualist beliefs. In fact she regarded all mediums as cranks or imposters.

Then, one day, she developed a serious thyroid illness which necessitated her entering hospital. Here she received her first psychic experience. To her amazement she discovered that, lying in bed, she could "read" people's lives as they passed by. She prophesied that the ward sister would be leaving the hospital for good within the next three weeks. The sister laughed at the idea as she had not the slightest intention of leaving, but nevertheless she did depart, and thus my wife's prophecy came true. An occurrence like this could not happen without attracting attention. My wife soon became the object of much interest, and eventually she gave the hospital staff and some of the patients further messages which also came true.

On discharge from hospital, she found that her gift of prophecy developed rapidly but it was not until a month later, when we were

9

staying with a friend in Surrey, that her gift as a medium became apparent.

One evening we had been sitting quietly for some time when suddenly I noticed that my wife had closed her eyes and was to all appearances in a trance condition. Knowing how she hated sham of any kind I realised that if this was the case it must be genuine. Then to my amazement she spoke, not with her own voice but with a much deeper one, which said "I will come again". Immediately following this incident she jumped up fully awake, explaining that she had experienced a strange sensation and felt afraid. I overcame her fears and when we returned to London persuaded her to "sit" again. This time the voice spoke through her for approximately 15 minutes.

Subsequently the Messenger, whose voice was controlling her, told me that the visit to our friends in Surrey had been planned from the spirit world, and that he had been waiting to use my wife as his medium, but as he could not interfere with her free will, had been obliged to wait until her illness changed her state of mind. Her powers now began to develop amazingly; clairvoyance and clairaudience followed without any human guidance or advice.

The Messenger assured me that he would remain with my wife throughout her earth life. As we learnt to love and trust him, our curiosity as to his identity became intense. When I questioned him he replied "I do not wish to be known for what I was, but for what I am. If I must have a name, then call me the Messenger." He then told me that we must wait until we had exhausted our efforts to trace him with the help of clues he would give us from time to time, ending with these words: "Whilst you are searching for records of my identity you are treading the paths I once trod, and that should make you happy." This was followed by a characteristic comment, "Remember, you are searching for the records of someone who has been very patient with you, now you must be patient with him." This remark went home deeply when we later recalled the patience that he had exercised in bringing us to accept his philosophy of life.

One day he told me that he had been a prominent judge and parliamentarian during the reign of Queen Elizabeth I and a turbulent agitator for political reform, which, more than once, nearly cost him his life. After his death in 1598 a Reform Bill which he had sponsored became law. He also told me that he had been posthumously honoured, and his body transferred from its original burial place, St. John's Church, Clerkenwell, to Westminster Abbey.

In 1941 my wife and I visited St. John's Church, before it was destroyed by bombing, to see if we could trace any record of his burial. Unfortunately all evidence of burials around the period in question had been extinguished. However, whilst searching the crypt, my wife suddenly saw clairvoyantly the Messenger standing beside a pillar. Subsequently he informed me that this was the spot where he was originally buried. On leaving, she again saw him riding a white horse across the space that led to the church. At another consultation he told me that he had shown himself to my wife as a reward for our interest.

Finally we discovered the secret we sought, and were overjoyed at being able to complete the chain of evidence that we had been given, link by link, over a period of several years. We had searched, without success, books of the period in the British Museum and the Burial Records of Westminster Abbey for the name of a prominent Elizabethan judge. Eventually we visited various London libraries and found that the only name which corresponded with the information at our disposal was that of Thomas Owen. I then asked the Messenger if we had at long last identified him and received the reply "Yes, I don't mind telling you now as a reward for your striving and interest in me – I am Thomas Owen."

The Messenger's eldest son, Sir Roger Owen, erected a tablet over his father's tomb in the south aisle of Westminster Abbey, the Latin inscription of which is translated as follows:

To God Three in One
Sacred
Under this tablet Thomas Owen, Gentleman,
awaits the second coming of Christ the Redeemer.

He was the son of Richard Owen by Lady Mary, daughter and heiress of Thomas Ottley from the County of Shropshire. He from his youth studied English Municipal Law. He so shone in industry, ability and judgement that he was elected to the first parliament of Queen Elizabeth. For his service to the law he was elected to the council of the Court of Common Pleas with whom he sat for five years with outstanding praise for his integrity, equity and prudence. By Sarah his beloved wife, daughter and one of the heirs of Humphrey de Baskerville, he had five sons and as many daughters. Alice his faithful second wife surviving him, he died in Christ on 21st December in the year of Salvation 1598. Roger Owen his most doleful son to his excellent and dearest father, placed this monument of his dutiful piety and remembrance.

In the Hand of the Lord are the Souls of the Just.
And I am the hope of worms.

In August 1950 we visited the Messenger's birthplace at Condover, and saw the magnificent Elizabethan mansion which he built for his son in 1588. Cromwell once made it his headquarters. Clive of India also lived there.

We paid a second visit on 21st July 1951. This time we were allowed to go over the house, now used as a home for blind babies. How thrilling it was to enter an atmosphere of the Messenger's own creation. As we came into a lovely oak-panelled room facing south, my wife immediately sensed that it was the Messenger's own room, which he confirmed later. Whilst in the gallery overlooking the hall, she again saw the Messenger clairvoyantly. He was coming up the stairs leading a party of his friends. The women were dressed in lavish gowns, and the men in elegant Elizabethan clothes.

Since the Messenger first came into our lives, many and varied have been our experiences, both spiritual and material. We have learnt to accept his teachings, and become wiser and more trusting; willing to obey any request of his, regardless of the difficulties involved. His prophecies have always withstood the test of searching verification.

Soon after our first meeting I had to undergo an ordeal which was to serve as further dramatic evidence that the Messenger really was using my wife as a medium and speaking through her to me. He traced my life from childhood onwards, mercilessly pointing out my errors and weaknesses and telling me of secrets which only I knew. For the first time I saw myself as I really was, and not as I imagined myself to be. It was a devastating moment.

He ended by saying "If you wish to be my disciple and do my work, you must conquer your weaknesses and change your way of life, for I want you to be an example to others. Choose for yourself. You have free will and you will not be punished if you choose another road. Remember that you can never deceive me for I know all your thoughts." He then proved this statement by tracing all my thoughts and movements from 12 o'clock that day onwards; they were entirely and absolutely correct. Finally he concluded with the promise "My boy, I am going to show you the true path of life, for which one day you will thank me. The road will be hard, but I promise you there will be glory at the end. Put my teachings to the test and if they fail to bring you the happiness I have promised then cast me aside." There and then I resolved on a new life. Since that day I have put his teachings to the test and his promise has been more than fulfilled.

Perhaps the greatest proof to me of his power has been my own amazing cure. I was suffering from a chronic and apparently incurable duodenal ulcer, and several doctors had informed me that they could do nothing for me. I was unable to eat a piece of bread without undergoing torture. Within three months the Messenger had restored me to perfect health. Afterwards he told me to go to the hospital to be x-rayed. The photographs proved my cure complete. Since then I have enjoyed a new lease of life.

When I first began to do healing under the Messenger's guidance he helped me in a way that was beyond the power of any human being. My first patient was my wife who was suffering from glandular trouble. Finding it difficult to know how long I should keep my hands in a certain position, I asked him if he could give me some kind of signal when it was time for me to stop. This he did by sending what best can be described as an electric shock through her which I could feel quite strongly. On every occasion since then he has always given me this signal – a wonderful proof of his presence.

Since the Messenger first came into our lives I have had many consultations with him, my wife being in deep trance. One day I questioned him about my wife's gift of mediumship and he replied, "I must explain how I first contacted Elizabeth, the nature of deep trance, and my power as a spirit 'control'. I was directed to her by higher powers before she entered earthly life. I spoke to her of my plans and she agreed to co-operate with me. I was directed to her because in the nature of the work I wished to do it was necessary for me to have a medium with a personality similar to my own. I did not start my work until she was in her forties; until then she had been unaware that she had the faculty of mediumship. In God's plans there is always a right moment for things to happen, so I had to wait until the time when my work would be the most important factor in her life. Here I must pause to express my gratitude and admiration for her sincerity and devotion to me; even when her physical health was at its lowest ebb she never once complained of her task.

I chose a deep trance medium because I had to have a reliable channel. When in trance she is completely unconscious, so her mind cannot influence anything I wish to say. Her eyes are closed sometimes for over an hour, during which time she neither leans back nor rests her arms on the side of the chair for support. To remain in this position for such a length of time, then suddenly to return to normal consciousness, fully alert and physically at ease, would be impossible to simulate.

The proof that I am in complete control is in the evidence I give of survival and in my descriptions of the afterlife, my knowledge of people's secret worries and problems, and my ability to diagnose

14

illnesses, even of individuals I have not seen. I could give many more examples, but think that these are sufficient. No other spirit can control my medium without my permission and assistance, but sometimes I allow other spirits to speak through her in order to give people the thrill of personal contact with former friends and relations. Nevertheless I am always in command and can stop the conversation whenever I wish. No spirit can produce the same voice as he had when in his physical body because he is using different vocal chords, but sometimes there is an inflection of his own voice. I can only express myself within my medium's vocabulary, just as a musician can only use notes within the compass of his instrument. I am equipped to speak in any language, but there are only two that can be spoken through Elizabeth, namely English and Welsh. With the power at my command and with another medium, I could produce trance addresses in the most exquisite and sublime words that anyone could wish to hear, but I deliberately selected Elizabeth for her steadfastness and integrity, knowing that through her I could get my message across in simple words. Likewise Jesus Christ gave his teachings to the world in simple language.

I would add that one of the main factors responsible for Elizabeth's success is her well-balanced mind, which enables her to separate her outstanding gift from the mundane things of life.

I have often been asked why the standard of mediumship today is not on such a high level as it has been in the past, with special reference to the times of the Greek oracles. Generally speaking there is little difference. The historical references to the quality of mediumship in the Greek oracles when at the height of their fame are greatly exaggerated. The oracles were regarded with awe and respect by the people who wrote about them on account of their mysterious nature.

Although my powers are limited, I have greater knowledge than people on earth. I can see into the future, and into the past, and also into the souls of individuals where everything is recorded concerning their lives. Any specific knowledge I need is given to me by higher powers. For instance, I never know the exact time a person is going to pass over, but if for some reason this is important,

15

they give it to me. The following is a good example of this inspiration: it came in the early days when I was explaining to you, Stanley, about the laws of cause and effect. I was inspired to tell you that your brother would die before you and that you must take note of the cause of his passing. At the time it seemed unlikely that your brother would die first as he was in good health, whereas you yourself were suffering great pain from an internal complaint. In the event, your brother did in fact die first, but you had to have that message as a warning to you not to live the kind of life lived by your brother. Later on, when you were still suffering, I gave you another inspired message – that in your old age you would be a very healthy man.

I was once asked why I had waited nearly 400 years before attempting my earth mission. I replied that that was the length of time it had taken for me to acquire the spiritual advancement necessary for me to control a medium. I had, however, previously been able to put inspiration into people's thoughts, for all human beings can be guided by inspiration provided that they are in a receptive state of mind." '

Stanley concludes: 'For a number of years before the Messenger came into our lives I had searched in vain for spiritual knowledge. Now, thank God, I have at last succeeded and found a source of truth which through intense experience I know to be completely reliable. His teachings from beyond, which I have recorded in order to help others, do not interfere with any form of worship, but are a further enlightenment regarding life, death and the hereafter.'

CHAPTER III

The Messenger's Teaching

The Purpose of Man's Life on Earth

'The soul is exclusively God's creation; man, and nature, have no hand in producing it. It is our essential inner self, formless and infinite. The purpose of earthly existence for each soul is that it may be tested, strengthened, and enabled to progress spiritually. When we die, it retains only our good qualities, such as kindness, love and strength, so that upon arrival in the next world, after our testing time on earth, we are powerful or weak, rich or poor, according to our acquisition of these qualities.

The soul is also the storehouse of our experiences, which it assimilates and transforms into faculties – thus extending its powers and moulding its individuality.

Creative and eternal, it pre-existed and survives any organism it uses. The soul gives life to the physical body, which ceases to function when the soul departs at death. The soul does not age but matures with progress, thus its qualities can make us feel young when age is taking toll of the body.

The brain is the physical instrument of the soul through which it carries out the activities of life.

God creates souls but the task of moulding them is the responsibility of the individual. Through life's experiences you develop certain characteristics and desires which make you into a distinct personality. This creative process begins just before you enter earthly life, when you are shown in a vision the environment into which you will be born and some of the places where certain events important to your progress will occur. You are also shown the major difficulties you will encounter, the kind of parents you will have and the tendencies which you will inherit.

The importance of this vision is that it helps you to select the type of person you wish to become, and to determine how to make the best use of your free will. The ideal you set yourself is registered in your soul for all time and becomes your guiding star. Without it you would be like a ship without a rudder, devoid of ambition and incapable of making decisions. In the short span of earthly life very few succeed in fulfilling their ideals, finding the test of free will in a world of temptation too difficult, but there is eternity in which to succeed.

The pre-knowledge provided by this vision is erased from the memory upon birth, but when you return to heaven you will see the picture again and form your own judgement of your performance.'

Life as a Testing Ground

'Your ultimate goal is perfection, which can best be described as beauty in all its aspects. At present you are on the first stage of your journey towards that goal, in a world of temptation where your willpower and faith in God will be tested. In the spirit world there is no temptation, therefore in order to develop and to discover your real strength, incarnation on earth is necessary. The environment into which you are born will determine, to a great extent, the severity of the tests you will face. Reincarnated souls usually choose a difficult environment because they are anxious to progress quickly. The tests for new souls entering earthly life for the first time are much less severe. New souls are easily distinguishable from old souls by their superficial interest in life, religion and moral values and because they are less conscience-stricken when they behave wrongfully.'

Awakening the Soul Within

'Unless your soul is fully awake you cannot get the best out of life, because it is through your soul that you receive inspiration – the source of knowledge and wisdom. Your soul is like a lamp waiting to be illuminated with understanding and revelation. As it lights up your interest deepens, your senses become keener, and your faculties develop. Inspiration is the greatest gift from God to mankind, and is constantly being poured out from unseen sources. In order to make yourself receptive to this wonderful gift it is necessary to have a desire for goodness and to be willing to train your mind to become alert and contented. The desire for goodness is necessary because it opens up the channels whereby you become receptive to higher influences. An alert mind is helpful because inspiration often comes at an unexpected moment, and if you are not fully alert you may miss an important message. And a contented mind is important because any agitation or nervous tension prevents the easy flow of ideas.

You will need repeatedly to analyse your own character, to admit your weaknesses and to try to conquer them. You will be helped to develop spiritually through your conscience, for that is solely concerned with moral progress, and by your guardian angel who accompanies you from birth to the grave. Although your guardian angel cannot interfere with your free will, he can help you to control it, provided you are willing to co-operate.

In order to progress you must try to forget self. When you reach my side of life it will be insufficient to say "I never harmed anyone". Although this may be true, the important question will be "Did I ever think of anyone except myself?" One day you will enter a better world where neither self nor personality are prized; where men are wiser and live according to divine law. By trying to forget yourself now, you will not be a stranger when you arrive.'

The Importance of Love

'Understanding other people . . . their characteristics, their weaknesses and their needs . . . is one of the most important contributions towards a happy and successful life, and it must be remembered that the real basis of this understanding is love.

Love should begin in childhood when your happiness and development is dependent upon its presence. Later on it is just as

19

important, for whatever you love doing you will do more successfully, and the greater the love for your fellow men the greater the ensuing happiness. Even when other people are difficult to understand, your love can help you to maintain a sympathetic attitude.

It is important for you to know that you are all born to be loving teachers of one another. In order to be a good teacher you must not only be kind, but also very firm concerning things you know to be right. Christ was the outstanding example of this; not only was He loving and kind but He was very firm on occasions when it was necessary to uphold principles. Never fear losing friendship in these matters, for although your attitude may outwardly be resented at the time, inwardly you will be admired and respected. Furthermore you have a special duty to your friends in view of the attraction, i.e. the love, that brought you together, so if you turn a blind eye to their weaknesses you will be failing in your duty towards God.

The reverse is also true. You must temper firmness with kindness even when dealing with your "enemies", then eventually you may find that they will become your friends, and may never forget that it was you who touched a chord that helped them to progress.

Now we come to the difficult question of returning good for evil. I know it is not easy to turn the other cheek, but if you can retain your self-control when the second blow is struck, the aggressor might well remember that blow for the rest of his life. So through turning the other cheek you may have set him an example that he will ultimately follow. I do not suggest that you should act in a cowardly fashion when force has to be met by force in order to defend a principle, but that you should never miss an opportunity of teaching others an enlightened way to live; failure to do this will one day bring sorrow and regret. Always be ready to forgive, then when you enter the next life where all must be forgiven, you will not be burdened by regrets. The immediate advantage of forgiveness is that it relieves the mind so that you cease to worry. When you reach my side of life you are likely to find that the people you disliked on earth are the first to greet you with the hand of friendship. What then can you do but feel grateful for the opportunity you had to forgive and forget?

You all leave a legacy on earth by which you will be remembered, and which will bring you either joy or regret. It is not a legacy of money that is important, but a legacy of kindness. It may be such a small thing as a smile, or a word of encouragement to someone who was sad, or a little understanding to someone who was difficult. These small things that cost so little and mean so much will bring you happiness in heaven exceeding your greatest expectations. All those people for whom you feel love and friendship will be there to greet you. The plan of life is so perfect that not one link in the chain of love will be missing. Although you may have forgotten many of the little acts of kindness you performed, they are all registered in your soul and in the souls of the recipients. If you could only see the happiness of a spirit in heaven, with a multitude of friends surrounding him, you would not miss one single opportunity of helping wherever you can.'

Divine Law

'Divine law is the machinery through which God's plans are put into action, and the evidence for its existence is in the perfection of the universe. From planets to microbes everything is subject to this law. The seasons come and go and day follows night in orderly succession. The movements of the planets are so exact that their position can be calculated at any given moment. The lower forms of life equally obey this law, but less evidently.

With regard to man, the directing principle of divine law is righteousness, by which I mean man's efforts to achieve love, wisdom and strength. Proof of this lies in the fact that opposition to it brings moral and physical decay. All the wrong you do is eventually paid for in sorrow, and all that you do in accord with good brings peace of mind. From childhood to the grave your history is registered in your soul memory, and at the moment of death, which always comes at the right moment, you will see this record in a panoramic picture under the floodlight of divine law.

21

Your life on earth is short compared with eternity, but extremely important, for you have to face many tests within a limited time. There are periods in every life when existence seems distressingly tedious and slow, but these occur when the time is not yet ripe, within God's plan, for certain events to occur. Since you know nothing of God's plans and can see only one page of your life at a time, much must remain a mystery to you.

The more you understand about existence, the more you will realise that there is a power which controls events. No matter how carefully you plan ahead, you are unable to prevent certain things happening that you did not anticipate. That power we name divine law. It not only controls events in the life of man, but it also governs the lives of all creatures. If the grub did not become a butterfly at the right time it would mean death. If the migratory birds did not leave at the right time they would die of starvation. Such examples could be multiplied many times. The perfection of the universe should give you sufficient faith that even in the smallest detail God makes no mistakes.

Such is the power of divine law that nothing of any importance happens by chance. It is not by chance that you come to know certain people, for you are all messengers of God, intended to teach each other something about life. It is not by chance that you are born into a certain family – that particular environment will provide the special kind of experiences your soul requires.

God's laws are entirely just, you receive exactly what you deserve. You are free agents with full control over your thoughts and actions, and you receive in some form or other the results of them. Through the law of consequences you acquire a greater understanding of right and wrong, for each is followed by happiness or pain. If you steal, it registers the act in your memory and creates a mind picture of what will happen if you are caught. If you think evil you eventually become evil; if you love you are happy; if you hate you are miserable. Whatever you sow you must reap sometime, somehow, somewhere.

Through this law of giving and receiving you discover the real secret of happiness. Although you may find it difficult to believe, and even more difficult to put into practice, I can assure you that if you could give without any thought of self, you would never want, neither would you fear, for you would have an inner feeling of security that nothing could disturb. If you give help to an extent you can reasonably afford or manage, without causing hardship to those dependant upon you, that thought of love will rebound with blessings for you and your family. I can assure you that when you reach the next life your greatest riches will be the happiness you gave to the people you assisted.

In order to understand this law fully you must realise that God is a mighty power and that you are His children; also that He hears your prayers and is aware of your good deeds. To give a simple illustration: if you yourself were the father of a large family you would be very grateful to anyone who helped those members of it who were in need. Now you are all God's children, and He cares for every one of you, so when you help someone in need you are rendering Him a service.

Through the service you have given Him, He will in return be of service to you; it may not be immediate, but He will reward you tenfold when you are in need. God works through agents to whom He gives the ability to make things happen, so that it is from the love and power of God that your reward really comes.

You are all born with certain faculties and aptitudes, and if you are content to use these without being drawn away from your proper path through conceit, misguided ambition or selfishness, you cannot fail to make a success of your life. God has given you a creative mind which will stagnate if you do not use it. The will to achieve is also of great importance for it is the beginning of the tremendous effort needed to reach perfection. So achieve all you can, for it is better to tire through labour than to rust through indolence. The greatest achievement is progress through sacrifice. Take for example a young girl who sacrifices herself to care for an elderly person who is incapacitated. Her own spiritual progress is greatly enhanced and she also gives an important lesson in unselfishness to others.

Divine law may seem to act unfairly in cases where the wicked appear to prosper and the good appear to suffer. Yet even the criminal must be given time to overcome his evil ways through experiencing the consequences of his actions. Furthermore he may have dependants to support who disapprove of his way of life, and he must be given the opportunity of redeeming himself for their sakes. However, the rebound always comes. For example, you sometimes read of a respected man who has held a position of trust for many years suddenly receiving a prison sentence for fraud on the eve of his retirement. It was not by chance that his crime was discovered at such a critical time in his life. Divine law ensured that the blow would be delivered when it would be most effective as a lesson. Some may appear to escape the penalty for their misdeeds, nevertheless they suffer mentally from fear, so are never contented. What they cannot escape is the judgement of their own conscience in the world beyond, where it is much harder to bear.

In the spirit world we abandon our free will and are happy to be guided by divine law in all our activities. If it is unwise for us to do a certain thing, we are prevented from doing it by the law; this creates no disappointment for we know that the law is right. It is not easy for you to live in this way, for you are less conscious of the power of divine law than we are, but the more you try to observe its effect in your own life and in the lives of those around you, the more contented you will be and the less you will fear. You often speak of the "kingdom, the power and the glory", but seldom realise the importance of the "power" – the law that works to the smallest detail in your lives. Should you sincerely regret a hurt you have caused someone in the past, you may find that he or she is brought into contact with you again so that you have the opportunity of making amends. If in the meantime that person has died, he or she will receive your thoughts of regret and feel happy concerning your progress. Good thoughts always ultimately reach their target, whereas evil ones remain in the mind of the sender. Thus thinking, and acting, in harmony with divine law is the secret of happiness and success.'

Concerning Religion

'There is only one way to God and that is through goodness – expressed in the life you lead. Sometimes man feels he is missing a great deal by trying to live a good life; he little realises how much he is missing through not trying. I can assure you that anyone who is determined to achieve his ambition through goodness will reach the peak of accomplishment; that is, of course, if his ambition is within the range of his natural ability. It is a great mistake to think that a good life is devoid of happiness, for with it comes the stimulation of purpose, the thrill of new ideas, and the entire elimination of fear. No effort towards goodness is unnoticed; it is registered in your soul and one day the picture of all your strivings will give you great joy.

Love, expressed as service to others, is the most important thing in this life, and in the next. If you feel the need to pray, I would suggest the following prayers. In the morning thank God for life and ask that during the day you may be of service to someone. In the evening, thank God for His blessings and express sorrow if you have failed in thought or deed. In both these prayers you have refrained from asking for yourself, which is the essence of true prayer. The law of cause and effect works to the smallest detail, and therefore it also works in your prayers.

Many people find organised religion beneficial in helping them to develop faith and courage in order to overcome difficulties. The value of ritual and ceremony lies in their aid to spiritual thinking through communal worship and its atmosphere of reverence. There is no such thing as the right religion; all are good in so far as they help the individual to progress.

The key to all religion lies, not in ritual, but in one simple truth which can be understood by everyone. Jesus Christ was the greatest Messenger ever to come to earth, and the only being ever to live a perfect life. His very simple message brought from God was the importance of love, love for God and love for man, and His mission was thus to teach mankind how to live: in a word, goodness of heart. Everything He did during His earth life was a lesson to this end.

25

The power of Christ when He was on earth is the supreme example of greatness through goodness. Even though handicapped by physical limitations, He could do such mighty works as commanding the storm to cease, the fig tree to wither; He could heal the sick by touch or word and restore the sight of the blind. Such power, He emphasised, could be obtained by anyone who successfully modelled his life upon His own. Offering Himself as the eternal link of love between God and man, Christ demonstrated, by His own resurrection, the immortality of man, and taught that the link of love is not broken by physical death.

Some souls are so spiritually advanced that they need no outside help and are guided by inspiration from within. Everyone who has an earnest desire to be good receives this inspirational guidance from the spirit world – from "the Holy Spirit", if we prefer to use Christ's description and accept his promise.

I remember, when my time came to pass over, thinking how little I had achieved; a great many people think similarly. I was always a student of human nature, and although not a religious sort of man, I believed in God and endeavoured to do something to help mankind. Then, when I came to heaven, I realised, as we all do, how much more I could have accomplished, so I was determined to try and do for humanity what I saw I had left undone on earth.

As I said just now, Christ was the greatest Messenger that God ever sent to earth, but I too, am a part of God, as are all of you, and in my humble way it is my task to bring God's message to earth from the spirit world. For that reason I like to be called the Messenger. Before I could be entrusted with this work I had to evolve sufficiently to undertake it. But do not imagine that I am perfect – I am far from it. There are higher spirits who are far more advanced than I am, and of whose presence I can be aware when I need assistance. Just as we who are engaged in my kind of work try to help those on earth who will listen to us, so do we receive inspiration when we need it from those more advanced than ourselves.

Although I have been in heaven nearly 400 years there is much that I do not know about the purposes of the Almighty. However, with my greater knowledge and experience than those of you on earth, I try to bring comfort by giving proof of survival, and endeavour to guide you all so to order your lives that when your time comes to join us here you will have a glorious homecoming; free from remorse, and with a feeling of a task well done. I also explain how inspiration constantly flows from us to you, and give you the teaching of Jesus Christ in a form which suits your everyday life.

God, in His wisdom, sends His appointed teachers to the world at times and in places where and when the world is ready to receive them.

No matter what anyone's religion on earth, Hindu, Buddhist, Christian or any other, when they arrive here they all acknowledge Jesus Christ to be the highest soul ever to have been incarnated. There have been countless other high souls connected with all religions, but none so high as Jesus.

Jesus in reply to the question "Which was the great Commandment of the Law?" said "Thou shalt love the Lord thy God with all thy heart and with all thy soul and with all thy mind. This the first and great Commandment, and the second is like unto it; Thou shalt love thy neighbour as thyself."

However, millions of people lived and died before Christ appeared on earth, and millions of people have lived and died since He appeared, who have never even heard of Him. Heaven is not reserved for the members of any particular race or creed; and it is not what we believe that is of first importance, but what we have done on earth with the opportunities given to us. If we think of God as a kind, just and loving Father, as Jesus taught, this is in no way contrary to what we would expect from such a Father.'

Faith

'When Jesus Christ proclaimed the power of faith, He gave to mankind the key to health and heaven, for faith is essential to success in every field of endeavour, including that of health and the progress of the soul. It is true that education gives you a wider

27

outlook and appreciation of life, but you should never allow it to detract from your belief in God and your faith in Him. Only this kind of faith can give you complete satisfaction within.

Never let any argument influence your belief in God, for no matter how advanced you may be in the knowledge of life you will never know the answer to all its mysteries. Your life on earth is just as much a test of your faith in God as it is of your ability to resist temptation. The greatest danger of disbelief is that it makes you selfish and egotistical, for as a result of it you come to regard yourself as the greater power.

You will never be able, by discussion or argument, to prove the existence of the higher intelligence that controls the universe; the truth can be perceived through faith alone. When you express doubt, people may say "you must have faith" but better advice would be "you must learn to create faith", for only by so doing can it become a conviction and finally a power.'

Suffering

'There always will be times when faith is necessary, for it is difficult for you to understand how suffering can be permitted by a loving God. Let us first consider the positive aspects of suffering. The main purpose of life on earth is the progress of the soul, and success in this direction is generally more apparent amongst those who have endured some kind of tribulation. Qualities such as understanding, compassion and self-discipline usually develop as a result of pain and struggle.

All souls are in the process of evolving, and this entails suffering, in various degrees, as you learn how to use your free will. Although you may find it difficult to accept, I can assure you that most of the suffering in your world is the result of cause and effect – some past excess, some folly or weakness.

While it is important to have spiritual goals, it is also important to treasure the body God has given you. Bodies as well as souls have their laws of health and beauty; to live within these laws means

28

well-being and contentment, to defy them means pain and sorrow. The true value of pain as a warning signal is seldom appreciated.

Your body is only constructed to last for a limited period, consequently a certain amount of discomfort is unavoidable owing to the weakening of the physical organs during old age. However, this is often compensated for by a mature outlook and by faith in an afterlife.

You must also bear in mind that the good can do foolish things, they can be careless of their health, or impetuous when crossing a road and be injured in an accident – none of which has anything to do with living an exemplary life. God does not impose penances on anyone, all He wants you to do is to learn from your mistakes. And He inspires everyone who works for the good of mankind and tries to relieve human suffering.

A final word in connection with suffering. There are rare cases where an advanced spirit, dwelling in heaven, chooses a life of suffering on earth to set an example to others of how to retain their faith in God in the most difficult and testing circumstances. These people are distinguishable by their unshakeable good character.

You may wonder why a spirit chooses such a mission. I will answer the question in this way. Sometimes a doctor will choose a life of great hardship and danger in order to relieve the suffering of natives in some disease-infested area, fully aware that he is risking infection and even death. The spirit who incarnates to set an example of faith to mankind is in the same position as the doctor; they are both on a special mission for God. Their outlook on life is entirely different from that of the average person, for they both have an irresistible urge to fulfil a certain duty regardless of any thought of self. Whether they illumine the pages of history or remain in obscurity, their example is never lost, for they always uplift the soul of someone who was a witness to their sacrifice.

As I said, there will always be times when you will need faith to reconcile suffering with the nature of a loving God. God gives life and takes life. The way in which it happens is sometimes ugly, but to the passing soul death is wonderful, no matter how it happens. It is the gateway to a happier and superior life.'

Death and the Afterlife

'Death, like life, is an essential part of God's plan and is invariably a wonderful experience.

Some people assume that after death many souls are doomed to wander in a kind of no man's land as a result of past wickedness, and are unaware that they have left earthly life. In my experience this is entirely false, and I have found not a shred of evidence to support it. In fact, it is an insult to God, as I know Him, even to think that such a situation could be possible. As a rule, people who hold these views never think it will be their own fate, but always that of someone else, the non-believer or the sinner. Such views are harmful, because they create a fear of death, whereas it is a wonderful experience, even for the worst of sinners.

God would not bring you home without letting you know that you had arrived. Wise and sympathetic preparation is always made for the soul's reception into the spirit world. When the moment of passing occurs, you know immediately that you have left your physical body and entered a new body. Pain and suffering have disappeared. You feel invigorated and full of the energy of youth. When there has been the great pain of a terminal illness, people are grateful that the moment of death is so sudden and so painless. To those who watch at a death bed, painful or violent death will appear tragic, but it is frequently not merely by chance that they are present to witness it. It may form a necessary part of their experience of life, perhaps to make them think more seriously, perhaps to awaken in them a sense of compassion for others.

Physical pain has always been a mystery, and a problem, for philosophers and religious thinkers, yet, like life and death, it is an essential ingredient of God's overall plan for the evolution of individual men and women, of mankind as a whole, and of the natural world, a mystery which, as yet, you cannot hope to understand.

Happily, just before your soul actually leaves your body you are enveloped in a wonderful sense of security and peace; the realisation that some great beneficent power is relieving you of all the burdens of life. This will happen with great rapidity, for you are entering a world that functions on higher vibrations, where divine law takes complete control.

Vision, understanding and memory suddenly become widely extended, and in a flash of time you are shown a panoramic picture of your past life, stripped of all illusion and pretence. This is your judgment day, when you stand alone before the bar of your own expanded consciousness, and can assess the progress you have made or failed to make. You are literally your own judge and jury, confronted by a clear picture of such triumphs and successes, weaknesses, failures and wrong-doings as occurred during your earth life. Joy and sorrow alternate as you are presented with your "bill of life".

Immediately following this vision of our past life, the most wonderful happening in the whole drama of death occurs. Christ appears to us in person. We see Him approaching in all His power and glory. He speaks to us, giving us words of comfort and the assurance that all will be well. Christ makes no discrimination. He meets us all, Christians and non-Christians, atheists and agnostics, saints and sinners alike, because we all need His loving presence at this time. No matter what our lives or beliefs or failures may have been, we are all overwhelmingly grateful for His welcome.

Christ has always comforted passing souls. God does not leave His children to pass through such a moving experience as death without someone to help and guide them on their way. And who is better fitted to meet us than Christ who knows every language and understands every soul?

God's plans are arranged with such meticulous care and understanding of the soul's needs that He now allows us to undergo the final stage of our journey in sleep. Like the calm that follows the storm, we end our earthly struggles in rest and tranquillity.

31

This blissful state is a necessary period of calm in which the soul is enabled to adjust itself to the new rates of vibration and to adapt its mental processes to its new surroundings.

We awake from our sleep refreshed, self-reliant, and with faculties so alert that we know ourselves as never before. We feel ourselves in the presence of some mighty loving power that penetrates everywhere and infuses us with a marvellous sense of freedom.

Following a brief phase of bewilderment at the wonders around us, we begin to feel a sense of familiarity. We are home again in the place where we belong.

Freed, then, from physical limitations and from all temptation, the soul has finally become master, and goodness prevails. Of the many factors responsible for the complete change of outlook at death the most potent is that vision of the loving Christ, together with the overwhelming peace of heaven. Even to the good this peace is profoundly impressive, but to the evil it comes as a heaven-sent blessing . . . which, of course, is what it is! For having had the shock of seeing their "bill of life", they feel that at long last they have something to cling to. Never before did they dream that such a state of peace could exist. The wrong-doer says to himself, "Come what may, I must not lose this. I will never sin again." The remorse that is beginning to take hold of him will be sufficient to banish any desire to return to his former way of life.

The experience of dying is so profound that it causes a complete change of outlook and purpose, no matter how degraded the previous state of mind may have been. It is a change which eliminates all previous evil thoughts and desires, and is necessary for entry into a higher and superior world where peace, harmony and contentment are the foundations of life. The widespread belief that death does not change our state of mind, and that a person who has been wicked in earthly life must continue to be evil in the life to come, is totally incorrect. Indeed, it is most important to realise that there is no form of evil whatsoever in the spirit world.

In order to understand this matter fully, one must consider the nature of evil, which arises, basically, from the physical and material side of life and the misuse of free will. It is a state of mind, due to human failure to resist temptations such as greed, selfishness, dishonesty and the abuse of sex. It is in fact confined to earthly life and has no connection whatsoever with any power outside ourselves. In the spirit world evil temptations do not exist, there being only one way, the way of goodness.

The spirit world can therefore rightly be called God's House, and therein we must abide by His all-powerful laws. Like the wind, these can be felt but not seen, yet they are so vivid and compelling that no soul would dare to flout them.

Disobedience would deprive such a rash soul of all the benefits of heaven, leaving behind an overpowering sense of separation and isolation. In God's House we have no power except from Him, and we can only receive according to the way in which we express His will. Our earthly standards are changed; selfishness and greed have no influence, because wealth is not measured by possessions – wealth lies in beauty of soul. If we want to be happy we have to be good.

This, as we said, is your judgment day, in which you become literally your own judge and jury. Those who have sinned gravely and find themselves, upon entry into the spirit world, in surroundings totally unexpected and foreign to their previous earthly experience, inevitably are bewildered for a while and anxious to clutch the hand of anyone who will help them. All about them is the beauty of perfection which they will be unable to enjoy fully until they have redeemed the past. In these conditions, when evil people see the picture of the unhappiness they have caused to others their one overwhelming desire is to make amends, and the knowledge of what their lives could have been like furthers this desire. Meanwhile, ashamed to mingle with those who are more advanced, they seek first a place where they can be alone in order to think things out. Realisation of earthly failures and wasted opportunities now creates a fundamental feeling of unworthiness and remorse. Conscience, so often stifled during earthly life, becomes exceedingly active and gives the soul no rest until it is prepared to acknowledge its mistakes and wishes to make amends. This clash between the imperfections we have developed and the surrounding peace and harmony of our new home becomes so intense that we just have to put matters right. As it is on earth, so it is in heaven: a clear conscience is the secret of happiness. In a world where our thoughts are like a book, open to everyone, this fact is more than ever apparent.

God's laws are immutable. They cover every phase of life. Obedience to them is the only way to obtain perfect happiness. No longer do we have to deliberate or waste time in wondering what is right or wrong. As the flower unfolds to the sun, so do we freely respond to the influence of law, knowing it to be our infallible guide.

Through the natural play of devine law we eventually reconstruct the past, and exact our own punishment through self condemnation and remorse. There is no half measure with divine law. We are compelled to pay for our mistakes to the utmost farthing. We have to meet all those people we have wronged either mentally or physically. We must see the wounds we inflicted in order that we may realise the full depth of the injury we caused. These wounds appear real, but in fact they are mind pictures created by God's law and are visible only to the person responsible for causing them. As we progress, we shall meet these people again and notice that the wounds are healing. Finally, when our debts have been discharged, they will disappear completely from our sight and memory. This payment of our debts must be made not only to human beings but to animals also. The law is perfect in its judgment and decrees. Its ultimate aim is to aid the soul's progression and therefore atonement has to be made for any injury we have wilfully caused to any of God's lower creations. Animals we loved remember our love. They are there to greet us with joy, but the law also compels us to meet those we have ill-treated; although they have forgotten the incident, we remember it, and how we wish we had been kinder!

34

It is easy to be good in the spirit world owing to the absence of temptation, but this does not mean that it is easy to progress; for progress depends entirely on the debt you have to repay. Although you are living in beautiful surroundings you cannot enjoy the fullness of life until you have a mind free from remorse. Repentance is not enough, you must understand and feel the real depth of the pain you caused others to suffer. This often takes a long time as it involves helping those people on earth who are suffering directly or indirectly, in consequence of your actions. But you will be permitted to help them through inspiration and guidance which becomes a great joy.

You may wonder how a man like Hitler who was responsible for so much suffering in the world could possibly make amends, as it would be impossible for him to contact all the people suffering through his actions. Such is the power of spirit that he can contact them collectively. Even though millions are involved he would only have to concentrate on the one great crime committed for the effect to be felt by all concerned. If you suspect that his task of redemption does not match up to his crimes you are wrong, for a mind picture of the suffering of his victims will be with him until all those people he caused to suffer, and their dependants, have left earthly life. Even then, when he meets them in the spirit world, he will see mentally the scars of the wounds he inflicted, until he has progressed to their spiritual level.

The best way to understand this mystery of spiritual power is to think of how Christ is able to contact all the millions of people who pray to Him for help and guidance. He thinks of them collectively, and as a result they receive a feeling of inspiration which gives them a new outlook upon their troubles.

Since, however, after physical death, no spirit harbours any thought of hatred or revenge, it follows that in heaven the practice of forgiveness is universal, and this is a great factor in the healing of remorse. As I have said before, a former victim is often the first to offer the hand of forgiveness to a new arrival in the spirit world.

35

Meanwhile, having his remorse to bear, the wrongdoer has sought that level of company similar to his own where there exists a common bond of sympathy. In that level, too, there is love and understanding. Everyone tries to help him. Nor is he cut off from those he loves among the more advanced spirits and can visit them whenever he likes. Although only time and progress can release him from remorse, the surrounding atmosphere of all pervading peace will help him to carry his burden and from here he will start upon the upward path of progression.

God is a God of love, and to Him all souls are precious. He never calls upon us to bear a load heavier than is necessary for our advancement or a load heavier than we can bear. Thus He arranges that the revealing vision of our past weaknesses and failures during earth life shall be brief, and detailed memories of them eventually fade.

Happiness is the keynote of heaven, which means that we must dwell in surroundings where minds are at the same stage of development as our own. In this way everyone is fitted to their environment. All accept this arrangement happily for in these surroundings they find companionship stimulating and satisfying. In the spirit world we are joined by those with whom we have a link of affection, and meet our affinity or soul-mate from whom we never separate. We are all of us destined eventually to find perfect happiness and to ensure this there must be a partner – one's other half. Sometimes we meet our affinity on earth, but if this does not occur we shall find them waiting for us in heaven. We can kiss and embrace and experience a warmth of soul that transcends all earthly sensations. This is a wonderful time of reunion with those loved ones we always hoped we would meet again, and those we failed to understand are also there, anxious to assure us that the past has been forgiven.

The world of souls is perfect and in every way suited to our needs. There are flowers, trees, hills, valleys, streams, lakes and seas – beautiful beyond belief. We have time for activities and time for rest. We can do a thousand things that appeal to our interest and

36

enjoyment. There is no deterioration or decay; the very atmosphere is a tonic giving upliftment to the soul.

The first lesson we learn in heaven is how to love. If we have failed to love on earth, the opportunity is given to us to learn and make amends. We are so anxious to put things right that we find joy in undertaking tasks once foreign to our nature. Nothing we learn, on earth or in heaven, is ever lost; even the most commonplace task is an experience necessary to the soul. We are given the opportunity of enlarging our former interests, always providing they are good ones. Thus progress and knowledge are infinite – we live for ever and advance for ever.

On earth knowledge and power can be obtained through study and ability. In the spirit world you can only receive these assets according to your degree of spiritual progress. For example, I was not a doctor on earth, yet I can diagnose illness in a human body quite easily. Progression comes only with service, and the more one helps those less developed than oneself, the more one is helped by those more advanced. Here is a very simple example of an act of service. If, in your travels in the spirit world, you see a flower you would like to have in your garden, when you return home it will be there for you. A spirit with the power to do this would have registered your thoughts, and found it a joy to render you the service of planting the flower there. Through simple acts of service you prepare yourself for more imposing tasks. When you first arrive in the spirit world, service is mainly concerned with helping your friends and loved ones on earth, because this is your wish.

Distance is no barrier in heaven – travelling is instantaneous. We only have to think of ourselves in a certain place and we are there immediately. Everyone has the power of thought in heaven, as on earth, but since thoughts are visible in heaven speech becomes unnecessary. You will have a home because of the importance of such a place to you mentally, but in time it will cease to be a necessity, and becomes a place where you meet your friends.

There is no compulsion to do anything, but the desire to serve is overwhelming for you possess unlimited energy. There is work for

37

one and all, because everything in the universe needs attention, from the movement of the stars to the growth in nature. There is also the uplifting occupation of meeting souls returning home from earthly life.

Time has no meaning now, so studies and interests started on earth can be pursued at leisure, especially those that give the greatest satisfaction and usefulness. Nothing is witheld from you that you have earned through love. For instance, if you are a lover of music and wish to play a certain instrument of which you have had no previous experience, the opportunity is given to you; you can play games; you can do a thousand things that appeal to you; everything in fact that you enjoyed on earth will give you increased happiness in heaven. It is wonderful to feel the powers of the soul increasing and enabling you to accomplish things you would never have believed possible.

Generally speaking, all knowledge is received through inspiration; if you need specific knowledge for a personal interest, you know intuitively which spirit will help you.

There is no fear of loneliness in heaven because you are all necessary to one another, thus the whole atmosphere is permeated with a feeling of true companionship.

There are no barriers, castes, or social distinctions in the spirit world: love is the ruling power so it cannot be otherwise. On earth personality is everything, the tyrannical ego predominates. It is a sign of your inferiority and proof of your selfishness. Your condition being so limited it is logical to suppose that all your acts would be centred on your own personality. But in heaven there is an immense association of spirits all harmonised together by the laws of a glorious affinity, each doing good for good's sake without any desire for reward. All work under the double veil of silence and anonymity, so that the merit and glory of their actions may have God alone as their source and their end.

Every encouragement is given to make progress, thus we can visit great souls whose presence fills us with upliftment, but we may feel unworthy to remain with them. Christ's statements "I was with

God before the world was" and "Where I go you may not follow" indicated that He belonged to the very highest level of company in the spirit world. But this does not mean that He is beyond the reach of ordinary souls less progressed than himself.

When the soul leaves the body at death it becomes very powerful and is able to create a body immediately. We not only have the power to form a body for ourselves at will, we can also create it in any form we wish, young, middle-aged or elderly; it cannot be deceptive for whatever we create is a representation of our real self. Because we have this power, we are able to show ourselves to our friends, as they arrive from earth, in the form they last remembered. Then, as they become accustomed to their new surroundings, they see us as we really are. There is nothing startling about this change, for they also see themselves as they really are. Christ demonstrated this power of the soul when He appeared to Mary at the tomb. In order that she might recognise Him He appeared to her in the likeness of His former body. He also did this so that the proof of survival might be recorded in history.

No man, still on earth, has been given a full vision of the heavenly world – it is so unimaginably beautiful, peaceful and perfect that if this privilege were granted he would lose all interest in his present life and want to go there at once.

It is significant that Jesus, who must have known more about the spirit world, and communication with it, than any soul who has ever lived, said very little about it. With His complete knowledge of human nature, He knew that the contemporary masses were not, as yet, sufficiently advanced spiritually for this knowledge to be granted to them. Besides, He was far more concerned with the importance of life on earth as a preparation for the life to come.

The moral of all this is clear. We should repent whilst still on earth, for by striving to put things right between ourselves we clear our debts. Motives count more than actions. We all make mistakes, but it is the motive which is important. Much that appeared to be of significance when we lived on earth, such as our ambitions, vanities and prejudices, seems trivial and even amusing when seen from a higher level. In time the progress we make wipes out unhappy memories of the past. We cease to look back because we feel we are necessary to the great power.

Divine law is the powerful instrument through which God keeps His House in order. It guides and instructs us in every phase of life. Under the power of immutable law everything is revealed. No longer can we hide, or want to hide, our thoughts. As we know ourselves, so in turn we are known to everyone else. Everything we possess or create, even down to the garments we wear (because clothes are worn), bears the hallmark of the individual. Deception of any kind is impossible. In such a world as this a degraded soul could never lift its head unless love and understanding were the ruling factors.

Love is the active principle and sustaining force, showing us God in all things, consequently we have no interest in other people's past faults and weaknesses. We only look for their good qualities. We live in a spiritual democracy where judgment is mature and everyone is advancing, so there is no general feeling of unhappiness, for we have all failed sometime or another. None of us has been perfect, and this creates a common bond of sympathy. The fact that we may see a person overcome with deep remorse does not make us sad, because we understand that the soul is progressing.

Slowly and surely we become aware of a plan of life that excites our admiration and quickens our interest. Awareness of God's loving power gives us complete confidence and faith in our ultimate destiny. So we triumph and evolve, moving ever onwards and upwards to more exalted company in a world free of temptation, where we find eternal peace.'

'The conclusion of the whole matter is this: the right way to live is to work and accomplish all you can. Never hesitate to do anything that will bring happiness to others and to yourself, then life is interesting until the last moment. Live each day as though you were going to die tomorrow, for then you will try to live as good a life as possible and will always be prepared. Love is the strongest link between heaven and earth, and the more you learn to love while you are on earth, the better you will harmonise with your surroundings when you come to heaven.'

Reincarnation

'Souls are created by God, and each is part of His divine plan. It is important to realise that, after their creation, souls remain here in the spirit world for varying lengths of time, before entering earth life. A young soul is one which enters earth life only a relatively short time after its creation and therefore has little experience. Old souls are those who have evolved either in heaven or on earth.

Reincarnation is a matter of choice for each individual. Souls usually reincarnate in order to test their strength once more against weaknesses they failed to conquer in their previous earthly life, and sometimes in order to perform a particular act of service, perhaps undertaking a special mission to awaken the instinct of love in parents whose nature has become worldly and hard, or to bring back love to parents estranged and drifting apart.

Rare cases occur when an advanced spirit returns to earth as a teacher, bringing a new revelation and giving an example of a noble life. A few, including some of the great masters of music, art, philosophy and the sciences, return to complete some desire begun in a former life which they have pursued through the centuries with increasing skill and knowledge. They enrich mankind. But the majority of people on earth are new souls – which accounts for much of the turmoil, tragedy, selfishness and almost complete absence of any spiritual ideals.

God seldom allows us to travel to earth alone, and therefore close friends in the spirit world frequently incarnate together. The same law of attraction that drew them together in the spirit world will draw them together on earth, though one might have been born in Australia and the other perhaps in Britain. When they meet, they at once feel a strong link and become life-long friends. Unconsciously old affections are built up again, for the bond of love unites us through all time and can never be broken. Real friendship is born in

41

heaven, not on earth. However, you seldom meet your particular affinity during your first incarnation, because you both need different experiences in preparation for ultimate unity. Each successive incarnation becomes more arduous, as the tests become increasingly difficult. This is one answer to the question "Why do the evil flourish and the good have misfortune and hardship?"

One should clearly understand that hereditary tendencies, and any physical weaknesses or handicaps one may be born with, have nothing whatever to do with mistakes in a previous life. Any wrong-doing one may have committed in that life has already been paid for by remorse, and no one has to pay the same debt twice.'

Guardian Angels

'Your world belongs to God and He has provided you with the means of finding happiness through service. He has given you free will, faculties and aptitudes to stimulate the urge to accomplish, and also a guardian angel to inspire you with the right ideas. This guardian angel is often an ancestor who accepts the role because he is partly responsible for your hereditary characteristics. Even those who are leading evil lives have a guardian angel, usually a spirit who once led a similar life on earth. Knowing the eventual sorrow such a life must bring, he is anxious to help them to conquer where he failed. Many things which you regard as luck or providence are the work of a higher intelligence, helping you. An apparently chance meeting with someone, an impulse to act or not to act, certain unexpected circumstances, on reflection can be seen to have met your most urgent need. Often what you regard as a bright idea is an inspiration from your guardian angel giving you assistance. For instance, you may hear of a man suddenly becoming famous through a new invention; his call to fame may well have been due to an inspiration from a former comrade, who helped him with the greater knowledge now at his disposal.

Morally speaking, life on earth is a conflict between free will and the voice of your guardian angel, speaking through your conscience. When you hear that voice, remember that it is the voice of someone who loves you.

Almost everyone, having entered the spirit world, desires to become a guardian angel, for a time at least, because he feels it is the most useful way in which he can be of loving service to God, and by taking on this difficult and often unrewarding task he helps to mitigate his own remorse.'

Some Questions Answered

Why are some people taken at the height of achievement?
Does the soul travel during sleep?
What happens to people suddenly killed in an accident?
What about apparitions of the dying?
Do the dead grieve over the separation caused by death?
What happens to the person who has committed suicide?
Should we pray for the dead?
What about our pets?
What is the nature of prophecy?
Do we, eventually, lose our identity?

Why are some people taken at the height of achievement?

'Not infrequently we are shocked to hear that some brilliant young man or woman, plentifully endowed with God's gifts, has been "taken". Yet we have no right to presume that such a person should be allowed to live longer than someone less talented, for God calls us all at the right time.

If we had only this earth-life to consider, there might be a reason for our presumption, but we must remember that life is unending and that no effort or faculty is wasted. We also know that the plan of life is perfect and God never makes a mistake when He calls us home. Furthermore, how can we be sure what these brilliant people's lives would have been like had they been permitted to live on? They might have ended in tragedy, illness or despair. A further possibility is that God needs them for greater work in the spirit world. In any event, what better time to go than at the height of success, when all men think well of you?

43

In the same way, many people find it hard to understand why some are taken in youth and others are allowed to reach old age. We should realise that every soul is born with a purpose to fulfil, and that particular purpose is far more important than our span of life. God's plans are perfect, and all things happen at the right time.

A mother who has lost her child at an early age frequently contacts him or her in the spirit world during sleep. Upon waking, the mother has no recollection of this, except occasionally the memory of a vivid "dream" about her child. Yet these meetings have been recorded in her soul memory, and when she in her turn reaches the spirit world, her child is there waiting to meet her, and recognition is immediate.

A child's interest in its parents does not cease with the fulfilment of its task on earth. From the spirit world the child will help and guide its parents for the link of love formed on this earth makes such contact possible.

The child itself does not suffer through death. It goes to a world infinitely better than the one it has left behind, where in an atmosphere of love, laughter and happiness it is cared for by specially chosen spirits.

Like adults, children also see their plan of life when they reach the spirit world, and this reveals to them all the facts about themselves, including why they were born to their particular parents, and why they were taken so young. So clearly are these things understood that they have no sorrow over the parting. If they were born to parents who previously had no love for children they are now able to watch the spark of love, which their birth created, beginning to grow in their parents' souls, and this gives them much happiness.'

Does the soul travel during sleep?

'The soul is a great traveller; as soon as you have fallen asleep it travels either to people you have been concerned about during the day, or to the spirit world. The only time it does not travel is when

44

you have a restless night. When it visits the spirit world you awake with no recollection of the experience, for if this were permitted you would want to dream your life away. After such an event you awake feeling refreshed and happy through having contacted loved ones, and good and wise influences. Many a person on waking from a deep sleep has found understanding of a hitherto unsolved problem through contact with advanced spirits during the night. These visits to the spirit world also serve another purpose, for as a result of them you are not a stranger when you come here permanently.'

What happens to people suddenly killed in an accident?

'In order to understand what occurs, one must realise two things. First, that at the actual moment of death everything happens at terrific speed, because the soul is passing on to a world in which we move on a much higher vibration. Secondly, that our soul consciousness is very much ahead of our normal state of awareness. So when instant death occurs through an accident, the soul knows what is about to happen a split second before impact – and leaves the body. The soul having departed, no pain is felt.'

What about apparitions of the dying?

'The explanation as to how apparitions of the dying are seen lies in the panoramic picture of our past life unfolding at the moment of death. As the procession of events passes before us, a certain person whom we deeply love may appear, as it were, on the screen. This appearance causes within us a strong emotional feeling which is directed towards the loved one. Then, provided that he or she possesses the necessary sensitivity, they will register a mental image of the dying person, often accompanied by a feeling that something unusual has happened to them.'

Do the dead grieve over the separation caused by death?

'No departed spirit grieves over being separated from those he loved on earth, for he now knows that the parting is only temporary. The reason why the wounds of separation take longer to heal on earth is because a sense of loss is necessary in order to nurture compassion in those left behind, and encourage them to think more deeply about life and death.'

What happens to the person who has committed suicide?

'We should never judge such a person, for we are ignorant of his mental and physical condition at the time of his act, and know little of his circumstances.

The majority of people who commit suicide do so because they lack the willpower to face up to the realities of life. They worry, perhaps unnecessarily, until the mind becomes overburdened and finally snaps.

God gives us our life. It is His, and any attempt to cut it short must inevitably bring bitter repercussions. At death, we see a vivid picture of our past life and its mistakes, right down to the final act. Remorse follows for the weakness we have allowed to master us, but in the case of suicide, motive plays an important part – if the act was unselfish, then the burden will be less heavy.'

Should we pray for the dead?

'We must not judge the dead nor consider ourselves in any way more virtuous. If we could see their souls we might find in them virtues lacking in ourselves. We should therefore examine our own souls before we criticise theirs.

We ought to bear in mind the fact that in their new world they are being cared for by an all wise and all loving Father who understands their needs far better than we do. Whether we pray or not, He will care for them just the same. Our prayers can have no effect upon God's designs nor on the departed soul's obligation to repay debts he still owes to life. In any case no soul would want to be released from his debts because by now he knows that peace of mind can only be obtained by working off such debts.

Nevertheless, our prayers are known to the souls for whom we pray. Our interest and remembrance bring consolation and warmth,

46

and if in the past they have caused us to suffer, they are happy to know that all is now forgiven.

Prayers, whether for the dead or for ourselves, must come from the heart – it is the emotional force of sincerity which secures their effect.'

What about our pets?

'The most important purpose that domestic animals serve with regard to man is to awaken the instinct of love in his soul. Many people who find it difficult to love their fellow men have a natural affinity with animals, and without the joy of these companions would never discover the link of love.

Apart from their use to man and participation in his mental and spiritual progress, animals also have a duty to fulfil in connection with the scheme of nature. This they unconsciously fulfil under the direction and control of divine law. They all contribute what is expected of them, nothing more and nothing less. It is true that through their association with man they become more affectionate and more useful. Nevertheless they are no further advanced in the scale of life than those in the wild state, for both are fulfilling the purpose of their existence.

It will interest you to know that some animals are clairvoyant, especially those associated with man. God has given them this faculty in order to prevent loneliness. Sometimes they see a vision of an animal companion in the spirit world; occasionally they are shown a former master or mistress of whom they were fond, and this comforts them. These visions are only possible in certain conditions and when spirits working with nature deem it to be necessary.

Through many incarnations animals progress towards the perfection of their species and the fulfilment of their destiny. The interval between death and rebirth is usually of the same duration as their earthly span of life, and they are always reborn into the same species to ensure the inheritance of certain faculties peculiar to their breed.

When you enter the spirit world your pets will be there to greet you, and through the link of love they can be with you whenever you desire their company.

No thought of love is ever lost – even though it is sent out to an animal with whom you have had no direct personal contact. It may be a wild animal, a half-starved mongrel roaming the streets, or an animal that was ill-treated by its owner. Even though such animals may be unaware of your love it is registered in their souls, so that when they reach the spirit world, and come into possession of their soul memory, they are anxious to show their gratitude to everyone who was kind to them. Animals do not register your thoughts, they sense your love, so there is no need for you to express this in words. There is truth in the saying "your soul goes out to someone" for all souls, both human and animal, are able to contact one another.

In heaven love is all pervading and is extended to all God's creatures who in turn reciprocate with their love. For instance, if you are fond of lions you only have to send out a thought for one to be with you immediately. There are jungles in heaven far more beautiful than those on earth, where animals live together in perfect harmony; you can roam about them at will, entirely without fear, and your presence will bring much happiness to the animals. Millions of these creatures had no direct association with man on earth, yet they now respond to his love, because they naturally respond to divine law.

Although your pets greet you on arrival in the spirit world, they only remain with you for as long as you wish them to do so; like yourself, they also have been conditioned to their new surroundings and although they enjoy your companionship they are also completely happy when they are away from you.

When you enter the spirit world you acquire a new sense of values by which you must abide. For instance, possessions cease to be important because you realise that everything belongs to God. This applies to your pets too; you cease to regard them as possessions. With this new outlook there comes a soul-awakening and a variety of interests with which to absorb the mind, so that the need for an animal's companionship is lessened. You also realise that the main purpose of their existence was fulfilled on earth. So when you no longer need your pets' companionship, and the time comes for the final parting, this causes no sorrow. You know that, like yourself, your pets are progressing towards their ultimate goal. Sensing this, the animals feel no sadness either. The chapter thus ends with both having learned something from the other which contributed to their mutual benefit.'

What is the nature of prophecy?

'Prophecy interests you more than it does us. You will not understand it fully until you reach the spirit world, and then you will be completely absorbed in the present and be happy to leave your future in God's care.

To put it as simply as possible I will explain prophecy in this way: God has planned the universe and everything it contains, including a plan for each one of you, which you carry in your soul. In this plan are the important events that will take place in your life in order to influence your progress. Although, through divine law, that is through the law of cause and effect, something is always happening that affects your circumstances and outlook, God's plan for you does not change. When that plan was originally made it was foreseen what your reactions to life would be.

Now, when we contact you, we can see your plan because we can see your soul, and therefore can prophesy with accuracy what the major events in your life will be. We can also prophesy the less important things in your life because they are registered in the radiations which surround your soul. Nevertheless, we are guided by divine law as to what information we should give you.

When I first began my work with Elizabeth Bedford, I would occasionally inspire her with knowledge of the future. For instance, one evening she was sitting with her husband by the fireside and their cat was lying contentedly on the rug between them. Suddenly, looking at the cat, she said to her husband "Within two weeks he will be dead, I have just seen him lying in a little coffin." Exactly two weeks from that day her prophecy came true. At the time there was nothing to suggest that the cat would die so soon, for he was quite healthy, but I could foresee this happening, and therefore gave it to Elizabeth, in symbolic form of course, and inspired her regarding the time it would happen.

Generally speaking, people who crave for prophecy have a streak of weakness in their character and a fear of the future. It is my mission to eliminate fear by teaching about life, so I only prophesy when it is necessary to warn someone regarding the future consequences, should they continue their present way of life, or to help a person out of a difficulty when they are doing their best to lead a good life. Knowledge of future events may sometimes reveal alarming details, so that frequently one is better off without that knowledge.

With the mystery of prophecy comes the question "How can free will be reconciled with a future preordained?" Your future is foreseen by us in the spirit world, but your free will is not affected. Although it is foreseen how you will react to life, you need experience in a world of temptation so that you may know and understand yourself completely. You are like children sitting for an examination; we in the spirit world know beforehand what the results will be, because we know your capabilities and decisions.'

Do we, at long last, lose our identity?

'Even in heaven the powers of the soul do not come as a gift. To be great, we must be good, clear of mind and resolute of purpose. There is no element of chance. We all have equal opportunity of attainment. When souls eventually reach perfection they do not lose their identity, as is sometimes suggested. They are at one with God.'

CHAPTER IV

The Link of Love
in Human Experience: I

THE MESSENGER INSISTS THAT THERE EXISTS in all of us a thread, a link of love which binds us for ever to God and to those whom we seem, but only seem, to have lost through physical death. The vast majority of us westerners, however, surrounded as we are by materialism, have lost all awareness of this basic and vital link, which, if it could successfully be taught and developed, would undoubtedly save the world from the dangers which now threaten it. Nor could there be found, surely, one single human being, however depraved, even among the monsters of history, in whom some spark of caring love did not exist; nor one who, in his life-time, had not experienced some small evidential happening, unexpected, unexplained and perhaps unrecognised, which, if he would but consider it, is in reality a tiny shaft of light from the unseen, travelling along the unresearched wavelengths of God's love.

These shafts of light may take the form of warnings, deliverance from danger, messages from beyond the grave, telepathy, strange coincidences and, above all, answers to prayer. Some few are spectacular, while the great majority, because of their apparent unimportance, are undervalued by the mind and soon discarded by the memory. The important thing, however, is that they do occur and should be recognised for what they are. Some typical examples follow.

Surely never before in the world's history has the link of love between God and man been more clearly, and more widely, demonstrated than through what is now known as the ministry of healing, channelled to us through the selfless dedication of an ever-increasing number of men and women.

In his book *Heal the Sick* (Methuen, 1924), James Moore Hickson, an Englishman born in 1882, records how at the age of 14 'we were sitting together one evening in the drawing room, and a little cousin was suffering acutely from neuralgia and in a simple way I was asking our Lord to help her, when it suddenly came into my mind, almost as though the words had been spoken, "lay your hands on her face", and I immediately did so, with the result that the pain vanished. A few days later I was similarly impressed to lay hands on the face of her sister, who had St. Vitus's dance, and the cure was immediate.' This was clearly an inspiration from above, expressed in the form of a command.

He owed much, he said, to his mother 'who taught me to pray and made the person and presence of Our Lord real to me . . . the most precious gift a mother can give to her child, for it becomes the foundation of one's whole life . . . we used to pray together as a family, for those who were sick . . .'

From then on, his life became increasingly dedicated to healing the sick through preaching, prayer and the laying on of hands. Guided to visit the Island of Iona, he was impressed in no uncertain way that he was to go round the world healing the sick and preaching the Gospel of Love – 'I knew it was a call from God and that I must obey.'

As soon as the Great War ended, therefore, he set out on his five year missionary tour round the world, visiting the U.S.A., Canada, India, China, Japan, the Philippine Islands, Egypt, Palestine, South Africa, Rhodesia, Australia, Tasmania and New Zealand, everywhere received with open arms; in the Far East especially he preached and ministered to enormous congregations, sometimes, it is said, up to 25,000 in number, who flocked to him regardless of colour, creed or nationality, and he healed great numbers of sick people. But it must be repeated that at all times and in all places his message was the love of God for us His children, and that through Christ He still heals us just as He did so long ago in Palestine.

Among the countless letters he received from bishops and church leaders, as well as from simple uneducated people, is one from the metropolitan of all India :–

Calcutta
Good Friday, 1921

Dear Mr Hickson,

. . . . . .

. . . the spiritual results of your Mission are more striking than the physical benefits which have been received, striking as in many cases these latter have been. They amply justify your claim that your work is on the spiritual plane and is spiritual healing. The living Christ has, I am sure, been made much more real to many . . . thanking you for all the help, spiritual and physical, which you have been the means of bringing to my people.

I remain,
Yours very gratefully and sincerely,
Foss Calcutta

James Moore Hickson was followed, in this link of love through divine healing, by the Revd John Maillard, who, early in his ministry, received a vision of the healing Saviour. In his first book *Healing in the Name of Jesus* (Hodder and Stoughton, 1936), he writes : '. . . whilst I was praying . . . one by one . . . for some of the sick to whom I was to take the Holy Communion . . . I saw Our Lord in the midst of them, with His hands behind His back, looking upon them with great tenderness and love. Presently He began to turn, and then I knew why His hands were behind Him. They were tied. The interpretation of the vision came swiftly. The hands which wanted to touch and heal the sick were held back by the unbelief of the Church. Christ was not free to heal.'

John Maillard, too, was fortunate in having a mother who was a woman of deep and simple faith, and one who knew how to love. 'To the extent to which our lives are moulded by our parents, I believe that mine was influenced most during the months before I was born. They were months during which my mother gave herself again and again to seasons of prayer.'

John Maillard lived an entirely God-centred life, healing many sick people, and is one of the great names among those to whom we owe the revival of divine healing. He also published his message in at least two books.

Dorothy Kerin, born in 1891 into a deeply loving and religious home, became ill with various respiratory diseases and remained so for nine years, for the last five of which she was completely bed-ridden. During this time she suffered from diptheria, pneumonia, pleurisy and phthisis, severe haemorrhage of the lungs, blindness, tubercular meningitis, diabetes and other ailments, was treated by over 14 different doctors, and finally became so ill that all hope for her life was despaired of. For the last fortnight she remained in a coma and finally, when death was expected at any moment and the Sacrament was being administered, she got out of bed unaided, and, unaccompanied, went down two flights of stairs to the kitchen, where she made herself a meal which included meat and was topped up by pickled walnuts. We say 'unaided and unaccompanied' because the 16 people assembled in the bedroom, expecting the moment of death, were unable to move for astonishment at the event they were witnessing. She slept perfectly that night and in the morning was able to run downstairs to meet the doctor who, not unnaturally, had difficulty in believing his eyes.

These events, the historical truth of which is beyond question, are recorded in a number of books, and, briefly, in the first of her own two books, *The Living Touch*, published by Wessex Press. As explanation for this complete and instantaneous recovery, she said that during her two weeks of coma she travelled in heaven, saw many angels, and met Our Lord Himself, who sent her back to earth with the command to heal the sick and give faith to the faithless.

Dorothy was instrumental, through prayer and the laying on of hands, in the healing of many sick and disabled people; she also established her now famous home of healing at Burrswood in Kent and was foundress of the Burrswood International Fellowship.

Among a number of others famous for their work in the ministry of healing are Brother Mandus and Harry Edwards in England, Agnes Sanford in America, and Elsie Salmon in South Africa. Each of these seven people insisted in their books that the healing power which poured through their hands was not resident in themselves, but channelled through them from above.

These leaders in the ministry of healing have been followed by many others. One of the most remarkable of those known to me personally is Renée, who, in addition to her gift of healing, is clairaudient. She is deeply religious, and a practical person, with a warm, friendly manner. I have seen numerous letters which she has received from grateful patients.

One lady had suffered greatly after a hernia operation, and developed a limp, in spite of medical treatment spanning eight years. Two days after Renée had laid her hands on her she reported that all pain had gone, and soon became convinced that it would never return. Nor indeed has it.

Renée has no medical knowledge, but feels that she is guided as she touches her patients. She always prays before giving healing, and reminds people that she is only a channel for God's power.

****

'My belief about healing', Renée writes, 'is that it's a manifestation of God's love for humanity. When I place my hands on sick patients I ask the Lord and all my friends in the spirit world to send their love through me to the ill person. I've seen many wonderful happenings. I never charge for my services, but I do keep a box for the blind. I've discovered that patients often wish to express their gratitude by giving to others.

I was first told of my gift when I took my mother to a faith healing meeting after she'd suffered with back trouble for some time. The healer, a stranger to me, said she saw blue lights surrounding me as I entered the room, and that I too, possessed the gift of healing. Subsequently, people would occasionally tell me they felt warmth when I touched them, and their aches and pains disappeared. About this time my clairvoyant friend confirmed my gift, and prophesied that one day I would give healing in church. I remarked that this seemed very unlikely, for I was not even confirmed at the time. However, about six months later a retired Church of England minister was staying near my home, and witnessed the relief I gave to his wife. Her foot was swollen and painful on arrival, but by the time she left me it appeared normal and was perfectly comfortable.

The minister was so impressed by this event that he told a friend, the Reverend Albain, exactly what had occurred. Mr Albain then asked if I would give healing at St. Dunstan's, Canterbury, and also if I would read the lesson during the service. I had never done this before, and the idea terrified me. However, I felt I could not refuse and read my chosen lesson forgiving those that trespass against us; for I know from personal experience that continued resentment can gravely interfere with health.

One of my most dramatic cases was that of an unfortunate gentleman who was lying completely rigid in bed with back trouble. He had suffered in a similar way on two previous occasions. This time the doctor had instructed the patient to lie flat on his back for three weeks. One day, in desperation, his wife sent for me.

I prayed hard for guidance as I drove to the patient's house. I learned on arrival that the gentleman could move only his eyes, and that a feeding-cup was necessary. His wife watched as I knelt and touched his leg. "Do you feel any heat?" I asked. "No, but I have some sensation" he replied. Then I pulled out the sheet from the end of the bed and saw his toes beginning to move. "Now you can get out of bed and walk" I found myself saying and, overwhelmed, his wife and I watched him leave his bed and walk out of the room.

It was for all of us a momentous occasion. I cried for joy as I saw for myself the mysterious and wonderful healing power at work. Later on I asked the patient's wife "Where did your husband go when he left us?" "He dressed and went to pray in church" she replied. The couple lived beside a church of which he was a verger. He was a very religious man, interested in healing long before I met him. He has since started a Universal Healing Centre.

Within a few weeks a friend of this gentleman telephoned to ask if I could see a lady who was on holiday nearby – the matter was urgent for she was in great pain. Her husband, a doctor, would bring her to my house. The lady had been confined to bed for three days, and had expressed a strong desire to visit me.

I started praying before the healing session was due to begin, and soon afterwards husband and wife arrived in a taxi. I discovered a lump in her leg of which she was unaware. Gently I touched this lump, and soon the patient began to walk up and down the room exclaiming "It's gone – the pain has gone". She told me that as I touched her she felt a warm glow, and that this was the first time she had been free of pain for four and a half years. She'd seen many specialists, and the possibility of amputation from the knee down had been discussed. Her letter to me reads "my leg is much better, needless to say, but my dearest husband is fighting an emotional battle. The miracle he witnessed through your healing gift has had a traumatic effect on his orthodox medical outlook. He is deeply grateful to you of course, and in time will, I know, benefit from the spiritual experience."

It is indeed wonderful when one can help people to lead a normal life again. One of my patients hurt her hand in an accident, and wrote a very nice letter to me expressing her gratitude. "Thank you once again for the wonders you worked on my hand. What a joy it is to be free from pain and to be able to grip things properly – so essential for my work as a nurse."

An interesting example of "absent" healing was that of my sister-in-law. For many years she'd had pain from her varicose veins, continuous pain, which made her job of running an hotel

57

extremely difficult. One day I spoke to her on the telephone, telling her that I was praying as I visualised her. "Put your hand on your back" I said, "now can you feel the heat coming?" "Yes, I do feel some heat" she answered, "and the pain is gradually lessening." Five years later she is still free from pain. My brother wrote "Mary's legs haven't hurt since your telephone conversation – we are still amazed!" Naturally it gives me pleasure to hear how my work, through God's power, can help people.

On one occasion I was visiting a lady who'd had successful treatment from me in the past, when her husband walked in. "I find it difficult to accept the idea of healing through the laying on of hands – but I do wish something could be done about my leg" he remarked. Ever since he was a small boy Tom had suffered from psoriasis on one leg, which so embarrassed him that he avoided swimming and always covered his legs when other people were present. "Try not to disbelieve" I told him, as I gave him healing. Tom was then 35, so the condition had persisted for many years. A couple of days later he called out excitedly to his wife that his leg was healed. The psoriasis had completely disappeared.

I'm well aware that it is difficult to believe if you have not seen or experienced for yourself. With regard to guidance whilst healing, I believe that through prayer my mind becomes free for inspiration concerning treatment – and I try to live as an "instrument" through which God's power can flow easily. But I also live a completely natural life, with a love for family and for material things. It is important to have the right values and a sense of proportion.

One day, when I was on board ship, the famous animal trainer, Mrs Barbara Woodhouse, came to visit me. A gentleman whom I'd helped had noticed that she was using a walking stick – and told her about me. Mrs Woodhouse had been in pain since July with a troublesome heel. It was now February. She came to my cabin, and after two treatments the pain disappeared. She was so pleased, particularly as she had a very busy schedule ahead of her. I told her about this book, *Love, the Eternal Link*, being written by a friend of mine, and she was delighted for her name to be mentioned, in the hope that others might be encouraged to believe in God's power through the link of love.

I would now like to describe the healing of one more patient, and tell you about a few incidents when I was able to give comfort through clairaudience.

A special dinner party had been arranged by a friend, whom I shall call Jane, in order to celebrate many years of happy marriage. She and her husband Jack had invited a large number of relations and friends.

Everyone was seated at the table enjoying themselves when suddenly Jane's husband slumped down in his chair. He had died instantly from a heart attack. For about 20 years he'd suffered from angina, but had lived a normal life and appeared in excellent form that evening.

Naturally the event came as a tragic shock to everyone, and I tried to comfort my friend's daughter, a young woman in her thirties, whilst her mother was being cared for. As I gently took her hand I noticed that the little finger was bent double, and commented on it. "Oh, that was injured in a riding accident in my youth" she told me. Gradually, as I stroked the woman's hand and finger, it slowly straightened out until her hand appeared quite normal. Several people witnessed this, and I was able to talk briefly about my faith in a spiritual power. I think this comforted many of those present, who were shocked and upset by this tragic and totally unexpected death.

Later on I gave much thought to Jane's predicament. That night, as always, I "talked" to my dead sister. We were inseparable, and have been able to communicate directly with one another since her death.

"Is there a message for Jane?" I asked, the very night of her husband's death. Into my mind came the words "Jack is with Richard, and is very happy". Next morning, feeling a little apprehensive, I repeated the message to my friend – who at first couldn't place the name "Richard". However, as she was gazing at her wedding photograph, she suddenly remembered that "Richard" was the name of their best man, generally known as "Fatty" for obvious reasons! He'd died two years previously, and his friendship with her late husband had started in childhood days.

So comforting was this message to Jane that the following night I repeated the same request to my sister. "Is there anything else I can tell Jane?" This time the answer came as follows: "Jack had a ring left to him by a much-loved uncle. It was lost once." I repeated this to Jane, and memories flooded into her mind. Jack had indeed been left a lovely broad gold ring, which he had given to their son. The son had lost the treasured ring, but happily found it five days later.

Now, I thought, I will ask my sister for one more proof for my friend, in order to sustain her and strengthen her faith in survival. That night I "heard" the words "He first kissed her under a tree". Jane was quite overcome by this loving and evidential statement from her husband – and she recalled the time when she and Jack in their youth, were strolling through some bluebell woods. They sat down for a moment, the sun glinting through the trees, and he lent over and kissed her – for the first time.

It is still a source of wonder that we can be helped in this way – you could call it a healing of the soul – and both Jane and I felt a deep sense of gratitude to the Almighty.

Finally, may I say a few words in general about healing and clairvoyance from my own experience.

Unfortunately there are some people who do not respond to healing. But you cannot have 100% success. Nor do you always know if a person has benefitted spiritually. There are no set rules, owing to the many factors involved. One person may be helped immediately; another will need several, perhaps many, treatments. It is all in God's hands, and I believe that if the time has come for the patient to die then neither healer nor doctor will be able to save him. But they can alleviate his pain, and often strengthen his faith.

It is important to acknowledge that many of us have reason to be grateful to the medical profession for their skill and dedication.

Personally, I need to visit doctors now and again, and appreciate their care. However, it seems that there is a need for healers too, and whereas drugs sometimes cause unpleasant side effects, the only side effect from healing is increased spirituality! It is often only as a result of suffering that we fully realise the benefits of good health, and learn to be compassionate and grateful. I like to give thanks for doctors and healers alike, for both are debtors to the link of love, whether they acknowledge it or not.

We should also realise the good which can come from all forms of clairvoyance, through which bereaved people are often enabled to accept their loss bravely and to believe in God and an afterlife.'

★★★★★★★★

Like Renée, many people have come to realise the power of the link of love. I have selected the following accounts from various sources to demonstrate different manifestations of this power.

★★★★★★★★

Within a Prison Camp

'As far back as I can remember, I've felt that there was an unseen power helping me. I always think of nature in this connection – the tides, trees and seasons – and sense that the rhythm and order in the visible world is directed by a spiritual force.

I never belonged to any particular religious sect, but it was a very important moment in my life when I discovered Paul Brunton's books on inner development. His books were to me a recognition of the truth that we are not just our bodies, nor are we our thoughts, emotions and passing moods. Deep within ourselves is the spirit, a particle of God. Paul Brunton's books, especially *The Secret Path*, have been my anchor, and I studied them carefully. They gave me the ability to detach myself, and to cope with any situation.

When the Japanese occupied North Borneo, I was put into internment and the experience was terrible. I needed all my reserves

61

of inner strength. I was in the camp for nearly four years – I'm six feet tall and came out weighing five stone. Our only nourishment each day was a handful of rice and some potato tops. All day long for one year, I emptied latrines. Guards were everywhere – there was no privacy of any kind, and we lay in rows on the floor. We were made to do heavy "coolie" work such as breaking up stones for road building. One saw and experienced appalling things like beatings and torture. The guards suffered from their officers if they didn't punish us – that was the army policy. Quite a number of prisoners died. Every now and again, perhaps once in six months, we were allowed to see our husbands for half an hour, but no touching was permitted. If we misbehaved in any way, our punishment was "no husband".

In order to support myself in these conditions I used to select one beautiful and inspiring sentence – from a psalm or poem – and hold on to it all day. I chose different verses in order to retain freshness, and this gave me strength for my ordeal. I've always loved "He that dwelleth in the secret place of the most High shall abide under the shadow of the Almighty" (Psalm 91). Another favourite is "Be still and know that I am God" (Psalm 46). This practice, I feel, will sustain us through all things, and has been my greatest help in life.

My faith has been strengthened through intuitions which have turned out to be correct. Faith in God, and a relaxed mind, enable one to be "tuned in" to the heavenly source of love. I also believe that when people are ready for it, they receive the guidance they need.'

Through Prayer

'When my husband and I first came to live in Dorset, my spaniel, a London dog unused to cattle, had to be found a new home where there would be no animals to chase. Some time after, I heard from his new owner that his back had been broken, and she, an elderly woman, whilst being unable to cope with him, nevertheless refused to have him put to sleep.

Unwillingly the vet (a farm vet) kept him at his surgery, leaving him for many hours on end alone and unattended. I telephoned frequently, only to be told somewhat abruptly by an assistant, that he was just a vegetable and a nuisance, and that permission must be given to put him down.

I was heartbroken, and yet realised that my negative attitude was useless to him.

Suddenly I remembered that my cousin had been told by a medium that her daughter, who had adored animals, was now caring for them "on the other side". I'd actually typed some manuscript concerning this, and I also remembered how, at the time, my dog often used to stand and look above my head – apparently at someone or something I could not see. I prayed hard that this girl might be permitted to help my dog.

A day or two later when telephoning the vet, I noticed a complete change of attitude in the girl who answered. She said that everyone there was completely baffled. The dog was just as ill and helpless as before, but suddenly became bright eyed and alert. She told me that it was just as though someone was with him, giving him the will to live. And, she added, the odd thing was that suddenly everyone in the surgery began to feel and act differently towards the dog. They began to love him, and felt determined to make him better.

And they did – they spent hours walking him with his back legs in a sling. Eventually (apparently a very uncommon event) the use of his back legs returned, and he went home to his owner and lived out the rest of his life very happily.'

Through Church-going

'Although I was taken to church regularly as a child, it was as a young adult that my faith became strong. When my husband and I lived abroad we attended church services as often as we could, and were friends with priests of many different denominations with whom we had most interesting discussions.

I have found that going to church brings a constant renewal of my spiritual values, and helps me in my daily life – for instance in my relationships with other people. The elevated atmosphere in the lovely building and the company of other worshippers, the flowers, the music and the inspiring sermons all take me beyond day to day concerns, and I emerge from church services better equipped to deal with everything, including myself.

When my husband became critically ill I found great consolation in the faith that I had developed, or been helped to develop, and each visit to church, where I frequently received Holy Communion, fortified me for the next challenge. I was able to discuss quite calmly with my husband, who also had great faith, the fact that he was not going to recover. We talked about reunions in the next world – with each other, with family and our pets. We knew that we would meet again.

After my husband's death following two years of illness, I had to contend with an awful empty feeling – but I was sustained by my faith and the kindness of other people. When I talked to the hospital chaplain who had been with my husband just before the end, he said that Johnny had told him he could see a bridge across the sky – and at the far side of it was his father, and friends who had died, waiting for him.

One evening about a couple of weeks after Johnny's death, I was watching a television programme which he would have enjoyed, and I automatically turned towards his chair to make a remark – only to find the chair was empty. But I was sure that he had been there. And in church recently, on Easter Sunday, I felt Johnny's presence next to me.

Without my faith in a loving God and in survival, I don't think I could have endured the pain, for my husband and I were very close, but in some ways, although life is difficult without him, I am fortunate, for I am certain that death is but the passing on to a beautiful new world of fulfilment.'

Through Acceptance

'On this occasion my husband was very ill having undergone a serious operation. "He's a very sick man; we'll have to be extremely careful", the surgeon warned me at the hospital. I returned home in a complete panic, and began to pray fervently. "Please God, don't let him go" I gabbled in fright. Then suddenly I realised that this was a wrong attitude – we have to pray, but we also have to accept whatever happens, however difficult the test. We have to "let go". I sat down and started to read the paper. A few moments later a warm and loving feeling surrounded me, just as if I'd been wrapped in a cosy blanket, and peace filled my entire being. I should stress that I didn't expect anything to happen, for my spiritual experiences have always come unsought, as beautiful surprises.

My husband recovered very well, and we had many happy years together.'

Through Simple Faith

In certain cases, where profound and simple faith is involved – faith uncomplicated by theological or denominational considerations – remarkable blessings can come down to us through the link of love. These have occurred in many parts of the world, in the homes of simple cottagers or the palaces of kings, in hospitals, or at great healing centres like Lourdes in the South of France. All, however, derive from a loving God and our link with Him.

The following two cases are taken from the records of the Chapel of Christ the Healer in Guernsey.

'Liz A. . . . suffered until the age of 40 from curvature of the spine. Repeatedly she had her meals off the mantelpiece, standing up. She would walk about with a hot water bottle strapped to her back, not knowing what to do with herself for pain. One leg began to contract so that she limped.

Ultimately a medical support was suggested, but a few days later after being fitted for this, she heard for the first time of the chapel, visited it and received a ministration. Though not a religious person in the conventional sense, she nonetheless believed absolutely in the power of God to heal her. And she was indeed healed, instantly and completely. No vestige of pain or weakness remained. On the way home she said "I could have jumped a five-bar gate." She enjoyed perfect health, started her own guest house and ran it for many years, helped at the local hospital and became an increasingly compassionate person.

Percy Le P. . . ., while handling stone with a pickaxe for the States of Guernsey, was blinded in one eye and warned that he must shortly lose the other. Moorfields Eye Hospital and two other hospitals confirmed that his blindness was incurable. At the end of each visit he was told "We can do nothing".

Possessing great faith in the love and power of God, Percy obtained the help of a local clergyman, who prayed that his sight might be restored and gave him the laying on of hands. Forty-eight hours later he telephoned the clergyman to say that he could now see perfectly, and in proof of this spelt out the registration number of five cars as they drove past the telephone box from which he was speaking. Three weeks later he passed his driving test, and not long after was granted a taxi-driver's licence which he held, and used professionally, for the next five years. During the 10 years which followed, however, he seriously overworked himself, suffered a grave coronary, lost the use of both legs, and became only partially sighted. But in gratitude for the original, and humanly inexplicable restoration of his sight, he has devoted all his remaining energy to helping others. He founded, and ultimately became President of, a charity which he named The Helping Hand, thus raising many thousands of pounds for the disabled.'

A Doctor's Insight

Extracts from a lecture given by Dr G. G. Macdonald, M.D., F.R.C.G.P.

'We know that we have five senses: smell, sight, hearing, touch and taste. These five senses are the means whereby we perceive our surroundings. I am now going to discuss our sixth sense, or extrasensory perception, which we all possess in varying degrees. Most of the time we are unaware of this sixth sense, just as most of the time we are unaware of the movements of our hearts, our lungs, and our intestines.

Extrasensory perception occurs fairly frequently in my own life. "Messages" come clearly into my mind – in words or in the form of intuition. These incidents are always helpful.

Many years ago during the post-war baby boom I was often called out at night in order to deliver babies. One evening I was relaxing on my bed when suddenly I received a clear "message" directing me to go to a particular house in Russell Road, North London, to see a man who had had a coronary thrombosis. I obeyed the voice immediately, and was there 10 minutes later. When I arrived at the house there was the usual clanking of chains and the noise of bolts being drawn. The door opened and the lady of the house appeared, dressed in woollies, a scarf, an overcoat and a brown beret. She was astonished to see me and said "I was just going out to telephone you!" I went upstairs and found her husband in bed. He had had a bad coronary thrombosis. I treated him, and when he seemed to be out of danger, I went downstairs to speak to his wife. She asked me again, puzzled but relieved, why I had appeared and then explained that they were patients of my father's practice round the corner from Russell Road, but that owing to his age they were reluctant to disturb him. They decided to try the son (myself) instead – and were about to call me. We had never met before, and I was unaware of their existence, and yet through the faculty of extrasensory perception I was given very clear instructions as to where to go, and informed of the patient's condition. The man lived five years longer, and his wife for ten more years, and they were my patients until they died.

On another occasion I was driving along to see a patient with bronchitis in Southgate. I'd had a very busy morning, and was thinking that probably I would need to continue my calls until late in the evening.

Suddenly I had a strong urge to visit an old lady in her eighties. I told myself that this was foolish, that I'd seen her the previous day, and was not due to call on her again for a month. However, the urge to visit this lady increased. I dealt with the bronchitis case, and hurried to her home. I went through the back gate and into the conservatory. This was my usual way of entering the house in order to save the old lady from answering the doorbell.

I found her lying unconscious on the floor of the conservatory with a Colles fracture. I went back to the car to get some plaster of Paris, set the Colles fracture, and then revived the old lady.

"What is the source of these vivid messages?" some of you may wonder . . . and the question is certainly an intriguing one. I do not think we can understand the phenomenon of extrasensory perception until we realise that we are composed of two parts – the material part which we all know, and the spiritual part which few of us recognise. We all consist of a physical body, and an extrasensory phenomenon which is called by many names such as the "soul", the "spirit", the "mind", the "unconscious" (Jung) – "the real me". This has been understood for many thousands of years. Unfortunately the great researches and discoveries of our material world have overshadowed, and made many of us forget, our own spirituality. The great chemist and philosopher, Paracelsus, in the mid-16th century, showed the new wonders of chemistry and said "These are great wonders, but never let us forget the importance of the soul of man."

Extrasensory diagnosis by lay persons can be accurate but is sometimes hard to interpret. I will give an example of this. Some years ago a lady came to me with symptoms strongly suggestive of serious trouble in her gall bladder. She went to a surgeon who removed her gall bladder, which contained a cancer. She returned home and was under my care. She became more and more jaundiced which suggested to me that something was obstructing the flow of bile. The surgeon reopened the patient's abdomen but could not find the cause of the trouble. The patient returned home, and three psychic members of the Baptist Church, to which she belonged, visited her to discuss the problem. Their verdict was that they could "see" a small piece of pipe in the patient's body which had been obstructed by a "piece of string tied round it". The patient finally went into a home run by the Baptists, and died there.

After her death, the Coroner for Southampton rang me up and wanted full details of the lady's medical history, investigations and treatment. He then ordered a post-mortem examination, and sent the findings of the examination to me. The cause of death was a ligature tied round the bile duct at the first operation, just as the psychics had diagnosed at their consultation. There was no evidence of a spread of the original cancer, and no other cause of death was discovered in the body.

I would like to tell you now about some of my observations concerning death, followed by a few personal experiences.

It often happens that seriously ill or dying persons appear to wander in their minds and talk to persons who are not visible to their attendants. This is very common, and usually happens when people are dying naturally, undrugged and free from any disease, such as a stroke, which might prevent them from speaking. Nurses usually write in their reports on their patients in this condition "the patient is rambling".

I will now explain my observations of this rambling as seen during the last 45 years. It is not possible to determine the constancy of these ramblings without knowing many dying patients intimately over many years. This is what I have witnessed :–

1. Patients under these conditions are speaking only to their loved ones who are already dead.
2. The patients are never in conversation with a mixture of living and dead persons such as they might do in a dream or in a state of insanity.
3. The ramblings cease when the patient recovers, and he rarely has any recollection of speaking with the dead.
4. It often happens that one member of a family, already dead, is chosen to perform the duty of looking after the seriously ill person, and comforting the dying.
5. This process is a universal one and has no connection with religious beliefs.

69

The following are some of my own experiences with dying patients:

I was sitting by the side of a seriously ill patient whom I had known for many years. He was not conscious of his surroundings but was talking and laughing with unseen people. I observed that the people to whom he was talking were all dead; his wife, his sister, and an old friend of many years. He was not talking to anyone who was alive, although he had many living relatives.

At about the same time I had another patient, a lady who was unconscious and very ill. I wondered if she would die. However, she recovered and lived about six months longer. When she recovered she told me, but did not like to tell her husband, of her experiences whilst she was unconscious.

The lady's father had died a short time before. She saw him at the foot of her bed on her left hand side – sitting down and swinging his leg as was his habit when he was on earth. He kept on telling her that she would be alright. On her right-hand side, at the foot of her bed, was her grandmother, who had brought her up from birth until the age of six years. Her grandmother also assured the patient that she would recover.

An old man whom I had looked after for many years and throughout his final illness, had always been frightened of death. I saw him at about 9.00 a.m. on the day he died. He was very ill, miserable and dying. Whilst I was with him he suddenly cheered up, and said to someone whose presence I could not detect "Oh, you are here, are you?" He talked with great animation and apparent happiness to this person until he died at about noon.

A patient aged 66 was dying of cancer of the liver and intestine. About 4.30 p.m. one day I explained to her younger sister that dying patients often converse with the dead. I revealed this fact to prevent her from worrying should it happen in my absence. About 1.30 a.m. the next morning I was again at the house, and there were present the two sisters, a lady friend of the dying sister and myself.

The dying sister suddenly sat up in bed and announced: "I can see my mother and father. They are wearing their ordinary clothes, and there is someone in white with them." I revived the patient, and the vision faded only to return two weeks later, when I was not present, just before she died.

In another large family, two members when dying, said "And Flora too !" Flora, who had stayed at home in order to look after her parents and had died from a pulmonary embolus some years before, had clearly been chosen to comfort and greet her own dying relations.

When I myself was unconscious in hospital on one occasion, I appeared to be talking to my dead mother. I was informed of this but do not remember anything about it.'

Recollections of a Priest

'I well remember that I was 11 years old when I first entered another dimension. It was during a Sunday evensong in church, where I sang regularly in the choir. For a few moments I found myself possessed of a far greater awareness of my surroundings than usual. The whole building was flooded with an unearthly, heavenly light. Deeply impressed, I told my mother what had happened and asked if it was a usual occurrence. She hesitated, then said "Just be thankful that you've had such a beautiful experience."

At 16, I had a finger amputated after four operations on it following a diving accident, and I used to chat with the other patients in the ward. One was a great character who'd been a newspaper seller in London all his life. He suddenly said to me one day "You're going to be a priest, David". "No, I'm not" I replied, "I'm going to be an engineer". But after that the idea of the priesthood started to take root. I went to Germany when I was 18, and visited Belsen which made a tremendous impression on me. I gazed at masses of large mounds bearing placards estimating the number of deaths which had occurred. Nothing grew, no birds sang, and desolate brown acres stretched before me. Although the temperature was in the eighties, a chill pierced my bones. I remember thinking that if the evil which produced such destruction controlled this life, it was a miracle that I was standing there with all

71

my faults. There surely had to be a power of goodness and love somewhere, to counteract everything I had seen at Belsen.

The night of my last examination in engineering, I had a most vivid dream in which I died – and even witnessed my own funeral. However, I wasn't in the least frightened, and as a result of this dream I've lost all fear of dying. It gave me a feeling of the eternal dimension of our lives. I'm sure that when we die it's not the end of our existence.

At about 22 I sought ordination. I felt that I was being "called", but as I hadn't been to university I told our vicar that I'd undergo the training with an open mind. The selection conference lasted four days, during which time I had five half-hour interviews with different people. I was conscious of offering my life to God, but wasn't sure of the outcome. I remember being thrilled when it was accepted that my vocation was a genuine one. Nowadays I leave myself in God's hands, and don't worry about decisions. I wouldn't have dared to plan my life the way God has done it for me, but I wouldn't change it for anything. I've always had a deep conviction that there is a purpose for our lives, but we have to accept difficulties at times. We do suffer from depression and many other problems; we do have doubts and need to ask questions. If we interpret life as ending at physical death we miss a great deal, and our standards remain those of the "market place", but if instead we have an eternal concept of life, our standards can become eternal. We should never, never forget the link of love which exists between ourselves and God. I believe that love has to be taught and received before it can be given out. Those in our society who have been deprived of love early in their lives suffer, and can cause suffering.

I don't think people always realise that in order to increase their faith they must work at it. Church attendances, meditation, expressing love for others by helping them, reading spiritual books – especially the Bible with a good commentary – all these things open the door to belief, and make us responsive to inspiration. Personally I depend on daily prayers and Holy Communion for my inner refreshment. If our faith is to be a live one, we need first hand experience of God.

I once knew a young man of 18 called Roy, who was dying of cancer. He hadn't had a Christian background. One July morning at 6.00 a.m. when the sun was just creeping into his bedroom, he asked the male nurse for a glass of water. The nurse, returning with the glass, noticed that the room was filled with a beautiful light. "Please put the glass on my locker" said Roy, "He's coming for me . . ." A few moments later Roy was dead.

My mother had pleurisy and pneumonia, following major surgery. In the afternoon we didn't expect her to survive. Later on she told us that she had seen her mother who said "Not yet, Vera", and my mother knew then that she would recover.

The work of a priest can lead to unexpected encounters. On one occasion I talked to the mother of a girl in her twenties. The girl had been attacked and nearly murdered. She was being strangled, yet her experience was not one of fear but of "heavenly music", and she said that she wouldn't have minded dying if this was what was awaiting her. However, she was rescued and recovered from the assault. "Never be afraid of dying", she told her mother.

I'm sure that one's own experience beyond the senses, considered with those of other people, can give us many insights, and these should help us to believe in God and in life after death.'

★★★★★★★★

My next meeting was with Rosamond Lehmann, the well-known British writer whose work I greatly admire. I enjoyed our discussion about extrasensory perception, and was impressed by the fact that she gives so much time towards helping bereaved mothers. Miss Lehmann kindly gave me permission to quote various extracts from her lovely book *The Swan in the Evening* in which she describes her own psychic experiences after the death of her beloved daughter Sally, at the age of 24. Sally had been happily married to Patrick Kavanagh for less than two years when she died.

A Mystical Experience – Rosamond Lehmann

'Nowadays I measure my life by Sally, not by dates. There was the time before her birth; the time of her life span; the time I am in

73

now, after she slipped away from us. The decision to write about it has not been easily arrived at; but I am not the first person, and shall not be the last, to undertake a similar testament, and like others, I can only go forward in the hope that the great glimpse (what can I call it?) which overwhelmed me at the peak, or nadir, of my agony may taste as unquestionably to others, as it does to me, of reality; and therefore will interest those who have had parallel experiences; may even just possibly (though I do not really expect this) rouse a faint query in one or two minds closed fast in the "intellectual" dogmas of negation. But my overriding motive is the longing to bring comfort to those in affliction as measureless as mine was when joy so suddenly surprised me. . .

. . . A fortnight later, a friend whom I will call by his initial J., drove me to Oxfordshire to spend the weekend with close friends of his and mine; I will call them L. and R. The evening of our arrival was spent in talking about Sally. All of them loved her dearly. I was unable to stop weeping; yet I began to feel, somewhere in my being, a tremor of relief and reassurance because they appeared to believe me, genuinely to believe me, when I went on insisting that I knew she was "not dead"; that she was "near me", "as much alive as ever" – scarcely grasping what I meant myself. At first I had been afraid that they were being merely kind and soothing; but when L. said quietly: "Of course", the tremor started. Later, when we went up to bed, she described supra-normal experiences following a shattering bereavement in her own life. Had she always been certain that life continued after death? Yes, always. Nothing more certain. Hers was the first voice to make me feel that I was not alone, or out of my mind perhaps.

But I did not, could not, mention the phenomena which underlay my urgent insistence on Sally's livingness. I was scarcely even examining them consciously. They seemed perfectly natural; yet at the same time impossible. They were physically and yet not physically experienced; appearing to occur in a body with perceptions which were mine and not mine. For instance, on (I think) the third night as I lay awake, I was . . . how to describe it? – lifted up: lifted on huge pinions out of my mortal dungeon; or perhaps a better description would be that a Great Breath blew me upwards, a giant bellows! . . . I had Sally by the hand and we took a great leap together. Another night, I thought that someone invisible brought her and laid her quietly beside me in bed. I didn't dream this. I didn't see her or speak to her; but an extended sense of touch informed me that she was lying beside me for some time. Another night, I became aware of my father, who died in 1928, standing by my bed with an air of wanting to address me urgently. He looked as I remembered him in his middle years; and the heart-wrung concern for me I sensed in him caused me to try, wordlessly, to reassure him; also to thank him for this desperate effort to come back on my account. I knew what it was costing him; I was as full of gratitude as of grief; and not at all surprised; and when, presently, he was not there any more, I felt a pang like homesickness; but also relief, for his sake.

Yet he had not "materialised", I did not physically see or hear, as L. with her highland blood had seen or heard. It was an interior happening. Needless to say, at that time I had never heard of the subtle or the etheric or the resurrection body; or of astral projection; or of the scientific likelihood that countless forms, worlds within worlds of them, are invisible simply because they are travelling on different energy levels, or at different vibratory rates; and because our physical eyes are designed as instruments of limitation.

To return to the weekend: that night passed, and so did the next morning. In the afternoon, my friends went out for a walk, leaving me behind to rest. As all bereaved people know, grief is inexpressibly tiring; and I was thankful to fling myself down on my bed and be alone; thankful too that in spite of feeling prostrated with fatigue I was still in a frail state of mental calm. A blackbird was pouring forth his whole being just beyond my window; and from where I lay I could see elm tops moving against an intensely blue sky in billowing masses of unearthly greens and golds. . .

. . . I was drifting and floating now . . . but where, and for how long? There is no way of telling. Perhaps for only a few seconds of earth time. . .

. . . Now I was with Sally. She was behind my left shoulder, leaning on it. Together we were watching Patrick. His face, only his face, confronted us; it was clearly recognisable but the whole scale of it was altered, expanded; and it was self-luminous, and transformed by an expression of dreaming beatitude. He was (we both knew) starting on a journey. I said "Aren't you going with him?" "No," she said, "he's got to go alone." I said: "I expect he's going to D." – (one of his closest friends, at that time a novitiate in the Dominican Order). Again she said "No"; and added "He'll go to Auntie Peg." This is the name by which my sister Beatrix, the actress, is known to all her nephews and nieces. . .

. . . Patrick's lit face vanished, but Sally and I remained together, wordlessly communicating. More than anything, it was like laughing together, as we always did laugh; like sharing the humour of a situation: his going off without her in some sort of state of disarray and unpreparedness . . . she made some characteristic joke (I can't define it) about the muddle of his packing. I did not see her. I had the unaccountable impression that she was hiding her face, that I was forbidden to look around. There was no light, no colour, no external scenic feature; only close embrace, profound and happy communion; also the strongest possible impression of her individuality.

Then, with no shock or sense of travelling, I was back in my body, awake, cheerful as if I had just replaced the receiver after one of our long gossiping joking conversations. I lay drowsily, trying to piece my "dream" together . . . then in a flash remembered. Now for the bite of the steel-toothed trap . . . Prepare, accept, understand . . . But it did not spring. Memory stayed in sweet tranquillity on the fringes of consciousness. If I was conscious of anything that I ought to scrutinise or question, it was my glimpse of Patrick. He looked so very splendid, so handsome and happy; why on earth had I thought him so shocked, so ground into the dust, that I had hardly dared to leave him in London and come away for two nights?

I looked at my watch and found that over an hour had passed. I sprang up, went to the window and looked out . . . and beheld a visionary world. Everything around, above, below me was shimmering and vibrating. The tree foliage, the strip of lawn, the flower beds – all had become incandescent. I seemed to be looking through the surfaces of all things into the manifold iridescent rays which, I could now see, composed the substances of all things. Most dramatic phenomenon of all, the climbing roses around the window frame had "come alive" – the red, the white. The beauty of each one of them was fathomless – a world of love. I leaned out, they leaned towards me, as if we were exchanging love. I saw, I *saw* their intensity of meaning, feeling.

I came downstairs to join the others. I couldn't think of anything to say except: "I've had a wonderful rest". L. glanced at me and said: "You look as if you had". Later she told me that she wondered if it was an hallucination that I suddenly looked about 30 years younger. . .

. . . That evening talk sparkled and rippled round the table as if the unimaginable death which had drawn us together were – not forgotten or ignored, but somehow overcome; so that we could tease each other and be teased as usual. No, not as usual. Our laughter seemed to bubble up from some primordial spring of well-being; like an echo of the laughter of the gods. I am not sure when it was in the course of the evening that I became consciously aware that the room was ablaze with light: a white column of incandescent light was vibrating between floor and ceiling – visible, I suppose, only to my opened eyes; but it never occurred to me either to remark upon it or to doubt that it was there, objectively present. Behind the dazzling screen it interposed, the faces of my friends occasionally seemed to dematerialise. I watched one of them, and was surprised, as well as touched and amused, to see that the countenance, instead of being on the square and solid side, had become almost transparent, and seraphic-looking, set on a long graceful neck.

All things were pleasure to me and nothing could grieve me. Truly for 24 hours I knew the mystical meaning of those words: still know it, inasmuch as that glimpse remains and always will remain enough to live by, in sure and certain hope that the end is joy. . .

. . . Sometimes – and increasingly as the months of the first year went on – when I opened the door of my flat, a cloud of

77

incomparable fragrance would greet me. What was it? – What could it be? At first I wondered if the old lady then living on the floor above me had begun to use some exquisitely perfumed bath essence whose echoes were somehow penetrating my rooms through the ventilating system. But the old lady went away, and still these exhalations pervaded all the air with an unearthly aromatic sweetness – spicy, yet delicate and fresh; compounded of lilies? clove carnations? frangipani? – and something indefinable as well . . . It was not for me alone this fragrance: I mean that it would, I think, have been quite perceptible to others; only, but for Patrick, I was so often alone in those days. However, I remember that Laurie Lee came in one evening, and after standing for a time in silence said three words only: "Now I believe". He had been one of the most passionately resentful of all those who loved and mourned her. I should add that he was acknowledging that the mystifying and pervasive scent I had mentioned to him was there, indubitably: I know nothing about his beliefs in the wider sense. As for myself I don't know by whose agency this sign was given to me; much less how it was brought about. I only know that it was so; and therefore, once I was sure of it, I murmured my thanks each time I came back into the empty flat. .

. . . Another mysterious thing during the first six months or so was the soft blue light, particularly in my bedroom. When I rested, as I often had to, in the day time, I seemed to be lying under the faintest, luminous blue mist, extraordinarily restful, like a healing colour bath. Around the window-frames and along the shelves beneath the windows it thickened and lay like a substance, as if an ethereal palette knife were spreading it. In the angle of the room, under the window, facing my bed, it gathered in amorphous clouds which I used to watch as if I expected (did I?) that out of this massed immaterial blue some spirit form might take shape and emerge.'

★★★★★★★★

Who could fail to be moved by this beautiful description of the link of love reaching beyond death, and its manifestation? This

78

theme is echoed in the following account given to me by a friend, Laura, who lost her husband. They had always shared a special relationship, and they belonged to a group which worked for unity among Christian and other religions. In Laura's story we see glimpses of her husband's expanded consciousness after his death. This interests me particularly, in view of the Messenger's assurance that our understanding develops rapidly upon arrival in the spirit world.

A Widow's Revelation

'Mine was one of those ideal relationships. I had met my husband at school and we became childhood sweethearts. Later on we joined an Evangelical Christian church, and God was very real to us both. We shared a great love for each other, and a desire to serve Him.

Shortly after the end of the war in 1945 we were married, and over the years had a family of four children. People commented on the happiness in our home, and my husband and I continued to share everything – our thoughts, our work, our recreation and our spiritual activities.

My husband died suddenly and unexpectedly of a major heart attack. At my daughter's house we sat and wept as we recalled memories of the happy life we had shared. But I knew it was God's will that my husband should go, and after a time I began to think about the journey of the soul and of all the spiritual books we'd read together.

One Sunday morning, three weeks after his funeral, I had an unforgettable experience. I awoke to a bright sunlit morning, and turned over in bed to say "John, it's a lovely day" only to realise that I was alone. "You fool" I said to myself, "you must accustom yourself to being alone." Then suddenly I "heard" a voice. It was so real that I expected to see John standing in the room: "No, you are not alone, I am here" he said. "Because you understand these things, and can raise your consciousness to a higher level, we can meet." By this time I was convinced that I wasn't imagining his presence; it was just as if I could see him smiling at me, and everything about him that was so familiar seemed to be coming through to me. I instantly recognised his mannerisms of speech and we carried on a conversation – I don't know for how long. He told me how much he loved me and how he had enjoyed our life together. Any differences we ever had were all forgotten now, he said. He was able to see things much more clearly in his new state, and understood people as they really were.

He then went on to talk about certain difficulties he'd encountered with one member of our religious group. There had been a personality clash which had not been resolved before my husband's death. I myself had felt that things were in higher hands than ours, but my husband had been bitter about the lack of progress with the conference centre, due, in John's opinion, to this man's attitude. And now, to my surprise, John told me that I was correct – he said "I can see quite clearly that his motives are right, which I did not understand on earth – and I can now influence him in a positive way. You must keep your thoughts on a high level for this will enable me to inspire you, and the group, towards realising its desires . . . I shall contact you whenever it is necessary."

John continued "I know exactly how you are feeling at present, and for a while I shall remain very near you. If you want to talk to me you can 'tune in' any time, just as though I was physically present. We were always so close and death cannot break that tie. I am beside you, and know everything that is happening to you; I can read your mind better than I could on earth. When you want to contact me go and sit in the spare bedroom – you will feel very close to me there." (This is where my husband used to pray and meditate: I have followed his suggestion many times and proved his words to be true.)

This first wonderful experience of John's presence after his death, and his ability to converse, even resulted in advice over my earthly concerns. He told me "I know you will miss me in the practical aspects of living. I enjoyed doing little jobs for you but now I shall send someone to help whenever you need assistance." This has frequently occurred.

Then I asked him "Can you talk to the children too? They miss you so much." He replied "I will contact each of them in the most suitable way. They may not be as conscious of my presence as you will be, but nevertheless I shall guide them. Tell them to 'tune in' to me, and love is the link which will bring us together."

In reply to my worries about our youngest son Jim, who lived at home with me and was pining for his father, John said "Tell Jim that when he watches 'Match of the Day' on Saturdays, I will be near him – we always enjoyed discussing sport together."

At first I couldn't bring myself to talk to Jim about this; he might feel that I had imagined the message. He and I had often discussed the purpose of life and survival – he was a serious minded boy, but like many young people, also sceptical. So several weeks passed before I felt ready to mention the subject. When eventually I told him, Jim replied "Yes Mum, I know it's true but I didn't like to say anything. When you went to bed last Saturday I thought I can't possibly watch 'Match of the Day' without Dad here to share the fun, but then I changed my mind – deciding that as you had to face things on your own now, I would too. As I watched the programme I suddenly felt Dad was sitting beside me . . . I know it's true."

For several weeks I enjoyed this intimate communion with my husband. Then came a time when John said to me "I explained that I could only stay beside you for a while; now I must go to higher planes; you must be brave and remember that I am watching over you all the time. If you have an urgent need you can still talk to me, and even if you don't receive an answer in exactly the same way as now, just have faith, and everything will work out for the best, although perhaps not as you anticipate."

It is 15 months since John's death as I write this. I have had my ups and downs, including two operations. The fact that John was not there to visit me in hospital was hard to bear, but I constantly take courage from his words.

There have been times when an insoluble problem has arisen and I have spoken to him about it. As he warned me, I have not always heard a clear "voice", but the answer has invariably come in a positive way.

I hope that reading this account will be of some help to others, who like myself, have had the heart-rending experience of losing a loved one, and I pray that you too may receive the healing that direct communion with your loved one can bring you.

I would say in closing, do not necessarily seek the aid of a medium, seek the sanction of your own heart; the veil between the earth and the spiritual world is very thin when soul rises up to meet soul with love.'

A Near Death Experience

When life, God's primary gift to us, is threatened by sickness, His complementary gift – the will to live – comes to our aid and when this is supported by great determination and a profound faith in the link of love miracles can happen, as illustrated by the following account:

'I have been helped by my husband to describe the following extraordinary event from beginning to end. I myself lost track of time, but shall recount the important issues and the ones which may be helpful to others.

It happened like this: I was a perfectly healthy, strong middle-aged woman happily married with children, and my first grandchild on the way, when overnight a crisis in the form of illness nearly destroyed me.

Suddenly, inexplicably, I started to lose the use of my limbs; I was rushed to hospital where the doctors, baffled, tried to diagnose my condition. We were abroad at the time and I was flown, with my husband and a nurse accompanying me, as an emergency case to London. We boarded the last aeroplane before fog prevented flying for three days. I was rushed up to the Middlesex Hospital in an ambulance with a police escort.

Four doctors attended me including a neuro-specialist. Finally they concluded that I was a victim of polyneuritis – in an advanced degree.

82

I was given an oxygen mask. My lungs collapsed, and I don't know how many machines were helping to keep me alive. Later I was told that only my heart continued to function normally.

Strangely enough, for 20 years I'd had a recurrent nightmare. In my dream I couldn't breathe. Tons of concrete seemed to be pressing down on me. Now that nightmare had become a frightful reality . . . I couldn't breathe or talk. I couldn't scream. I couldn't move at all. I was nearly three weeks without sleep; I was certain that if I allowed myself to fall asleep I would die.

I was given five hours to live, and at this point my husband telephoned Ampleforth, his old school, and asked if prayers could be offered up for me.

I could see, as if I was looking through polythene sheeting, and I could hear, but I couldn't move an inch. Suddenly I left my body. I was up above it in a corner of the room. I knew then that I had a choice, either to return to my body or not. I was absolutely determined to live, and I know that when finally I did return, it was with "outside" help. Twice I remember a vibration of "outside" help – and it came as I prayed desperately to Our Lady.

At one time I had a tracheotomy to help me to breathe. Everything possible in the way of medical help was given throughout my illness – but I needed something extra – and that was a combination of spiritual power and my own determination.

Immediately after returning to my body I knew that I'd beaten death. I could sleep safely now. A lovely warm peaceful sensation came over me; the kind of feeling a child has when its mother tucks it up in bed.

Then with every ounce of willpower I possessed, I concentrated on the act of moving my right forefinger. Very gradually, very slowly it obeyed me, and when a close friend visited me I started to spell out messages with it. At some stage a specialist said "You are going to live – you will get over this. It's a triumph of mind over matter."

I was helped by a lecture I'd attended in which a woman described how she had survived eight years of solitary confinement in a Russian jail. She continually visualised normal life, even packing for a holiday – and thus kept her sanity. I did the same thing. I love poetry, and thought about it, and mentally visited my grandmother's sitting room, and tried to remember names of school friends. I made my mind work extremely hard.

My daughter, with whom I have a special rapport, visited me, and knowing my love of children, arrived in a tight fitting dress and sat in such a way that I could clearly see her advanced stage of pregnancy! She knew that this would further my will to live – and it did! I was aware that I was needed, and was utterly determined to recover.

Two things showed me an improvement in my condition: one was when I actually smelled the steak and kidney pie which my husband was eating as he sat beside me (and I love this dish!) and the other was when I started to notice the flowers in my room.

This appalling period in my life had started in early June, and it wasn't until the end of September that I was able to return home, on a stretcher. In the spring of the following year I managed to walk slowly up and down the terrace pushing my new grandson in his pram!

My recovery was very slow – but I made it! I am immensely grateful to everyone for all the wonderful help and love that I received. Much later on I made a special pilgrimage to Lourdes in order to thank Our Lady.

What have I learned from this ordeal? I know that I existed outside my body – and that part of my "being" is entirely separate from my physical body. I know that I was given a tremendous amount of "outside" or spiritual help, and love from family and friends, in addition to the wonderful and caring medical assistance. The fact that the nurses talked to me all the time, calling me by my christian name, Peggy, although they received no response whatsoever, was a continual inspiration. I know that determination is a vital factor – especially when you're fighting for your life.

I now have a far greater consciousness of my own mortality, and the fragile thread between life and death. I don't take life for granted any more. The "awareness" I already had before my illness has increased one hundredfold. I regret the time wasted on petty worries and petty occupations, and appreciate far more deeply the real and important issues such as love, family and nature. A few days ago I sat happily in the garden watching a beautiful butterfly settle on my arm, and a thrush hopping about at my feet. These simple but lovely things now give me immense pleasure. I've been given back a great gift – for life is a beautiful gift – and I appreciate and treasure it with all of my being.

My friends tell me that my experience and determination to conquer severe illness and to live fully again have helped them with their own difficulties. "Peggy did it – so can I" is how a great friend expressed her feelings to me the other day.'

CHAPTER V

The Link of Love
in Human Experience: II

THE FOLLOWING PASSAGES ARE PERSONAL accounts of expanded consciousness which I have received from many different people. Those I have selected illustrate how the link of love can be seen to operate through telepathy, intuition, precognition, visions, dreams and contact with those who have passed on.

★★★★★★★

'I have a special rapport with my daughter, and we often experience telepathy, which on one occasion warned me of an approaching crisis so that I was able to deal with it promptly and successfully.

One night I was quite unable to relax and fall asleep. I kept repeating to my husband "I'm sure something is wrong – that Ann is in some kind of difficulty." I was extremely worried – we were abroad at the time and Ann was in England. Then the telephone rang . . . it was ten past one in the morning.

Ann, who was quite young, had been staying with friends in the country for the weekend. She had been put on a train to London that evening. She was ringing me – panic-stricken – from a telephone booth at Waterloo Station, "Mummy, what shall I do . . .? There are no taxis, I'm alone, and a man is following me – what shall I do?" I told her to ask the operator to reverse the charge, and that she must keep talking to her father whilst I went next door and contacted the police. I ran to our neighbour, informed the local police and they immediately telephoned London. A police escort was sent to fetch Ann, and all was well.

Perhaps because I was prepared in advance I was able to act calmly when my daughter telephoned.'

****

'I was on my way to a dinner party and had driven a short distance when suddenly I had a strong feeling that I must return home at once and telephone my sister to enquire about my brother-in-law. It was similar to the feeling one has if one leaves the house and suddenly realises that one has forgotten to turn off an electric fire.

I quickly changed direction and drove home where I immediately telephoned my sister. My brother-in-law had died some 10 minutes earlier; so I cancelled my engagement and went straight over to comfort and help her. At the time of this hunch I was quite relaxed while driving to the party, and was not worrying about my brother-in-law or his situation.'

****

'In Italy during the war, I was sitting on top of a deep slit trench waiting for an "O" group to assemble. We'd had a very nasty time since dawn, and people had been killed or wounded all around us as we were under enemy observation.

We had moved from an exposed position to a less exposed one, but tanks were firing behind us on to enemy guns. The area we'd reached had a couple of small houses near it, and was covered in olive trees. I had begun *I Claudius* by Robert Graves, and had reached page 64. I opened the paperback and began to read when suddenly a strong "force" urged me to get inside the slit trench. I will spare you the tragic details, but a shell hit a tree with the result that everyone in the assembling "O" group was killed as the

87

splinters hurtled downwards. I still have a slight mark on my left leg from a small piece of Baron Krupps' arsenal.'

★★★★★★★★

'I am a nursing sister, and my "sixth sense" repeatedly helps me in my job, but it is difficult to describe how it works with me; I suddenly get a strong feeling about something, and there will always be a purpose for it which I will discover later.

I don't question my sudden feelings; I just act upon them. Once, when I was looking after a patient with influenza, the doctor informed me that it was unnecessary for me to visit him again until after Christmas Day. However, on Christmas morning, I felt a definite urge to visit the patient, and upon arrival found him in a serious condition. He was immediately moved to hospital and eventually recovered from his illness.

Another time my telephone rang, and it was a child's voice telling me that a baby had been born, and giving an address on a housing estate. I asked the child to repeat this, but she put down the receiver. However, I felt instantly that something was amiss. So I went straight to the given address only to discover that it was the wrong house. When I reported the event to the authorities they thought it was a hoax call. However I knew it was true, and that there was a clue in the address. I then went to a house with the same number in a neighbouring estate, and immediately felt I was on the right track. A child answered the door, but the inhabitants of the house denied everything. As soon as I arrived, I sensed that sadly I wasn't going to be able to save the baby.

Forty-eight hours later a dead baby was found in a brook. Eventually the police contacted me, and I took them to both houses, having reminded them of my suspicions. The police then made thorough investigations and the matter was taken out of my hands – but I learned that all my intuitions had been correct.

I would like as a nurse to end with a few words of reassurance, for I know that many people dread pain and have a very real fear of death.

88

I have had much experience of help from above in the form of intuition, and have developed a strong faith. The medical profession have advanced greatly in their knowledge of how to control pain, and I'm convinced that we should not fear death. Many times I have seen a dying person's face light up with happiness as the end approaches. We really grieve for ourselves when we mourn the dead; the person who has died knows perfect peace.'

★★★★★★★★

'I was staying in an hotel by myself and entered the restaurant hoping to find an empty table. A gentleman was sitting alone at a window table. The waitress said to me "I'm afraid you'll have to share his table – there's nowhere else vacant." So reluctantly I sat down. After a while we started to talk. He was at a very low ebb, awaiting divorce, but we had a pleasant conversation and enjoyed each other's company. Much later he confided to me that the moment he set eyes upon me a voice said to him "this is your future wife." The story ends happily as we became great friends and eventually married – most successfully!'

★★★★★★★★

'During the time of our engagement my fiancé was working in the Far East. Suddenly I knew that he was on his way home. This was totally unexpected as he was due to spend a further two years there with his firm, Shell Oil. The following day I received his wire stating "Homecoming, Robert."

I had another precognition concerning him during the Second World War. Robert had volunteered for work in the navy. One day the telephone rang, and he was called up. As I heard the bell ringing I knew that my husband would never return – but that he wouldn't die until the year 1941. Then, during the very week before his ship went down, I knew his time had come. I was grateful for the warning I had received for it made the blow, when it came, much easier to bear.'

89

★★★★★★★★

'Although I was extremely close to my mother we had never discussed the afterlife. My mother was 83 years old, and she'd had a bad heart for some time – but there was no change in her condition at the time of the following event:

One night I awoke and noticed that her light was on, so I went into her bedroom. "Now I want you to be sensible about this" she said, "I'm not going to be with you very much longer – they're all waiting for me, and I don't want you to hold me back. I want to go on my journey."

About 10 days later she was having tea with my sister. They were chatting, and my sister was refilling my mother's cup when she heard a slight sigh. She looked up and realised that my mother had died.'

★★★★★★★★

'I am a doctor. On one occasion I was looking after an old gentleman in a coma. He was estranged from his daughter, bitter because he felt her attitude was unjustified, and angry because he could do nothing, although in fact he intended to do nothing to heal the rift. Eventually he changed his mind and asked to see her – but she consistently refused to be reconciled to a man whom she had come to despise. The old gentleman then went into a coma, and filled with remorse she came to the hospice apparently too late to converse with him.

On bending down to speak to the man, who was in a deep coma, she somehow communicated with him; he awoke, sat up in bed and ate a hearty breakfast at three in the morning; and continued to eat, drink, laugh and share great happiness with her throughout the day until she left, as she had to, the following night.

Immediately after she had gone I chatted to the patient, saying "See you in the morning", as indeed I expected to do, in view of the fact that he had recovered from his coma and was now in such

90

excellent spirits. But he replied "No, doctor, my life's work is now complete. Thank you for all you've done," and died shortly afterwards.

Many patients, particularly in the older generation, have a deep and accurate inner sense of when they are going to die. And it is not uncommon for a patient to tell us that he or she is about to die, and do so within 12 to 24 hours.'

★★★★★★★

'At the age of 13 months my little boy died – through the mysterious cot death syndrome. I was totally shattered, and later on my mother told me that I kept repeating "Mum, where is he? I don't know if he's alright."

Three days after Martin's death my mother and I had supper together. She, too, had been in a state of great distress, weighed down with sorrow, but I noticed immediately that there was a marked change in her for the better. She was most insistent that I should listen carefully to her. "I must tell you," she said, "I have seen Martin." It transpired that she was sitting quietly alone in her room praying when she had the following vision: she saw my son crawling along, smiling, and waving happily (he had just learnt to wave). He was wearing a little pale blue suit, she told me, which accentuated his lovely blue eyes. I felt greatly comforted as she stressed how happy Martin had appeared, and this sustained me through an appallingly difficult time.

Later on I became more deeply interested in the subject of survival of death, and read many of the relevant books. One of these contained a clairvoyant's description of the clothes worn by a drowning man. It then came to me in a flash that my real evidence also lay in the clothes, for I was convinced that my mother had never seen Martin wearing his pale blue night suit which had been a recent acquisition.

The weekend before Martin died, my husband and I had been staying with my mother in a cottage adjoining the main house. She was feeling very low at the time, and never visited my son in bed. She saw him only during the daytime, crawling about in dark blue or red day clothes given to him by his other grandmother. So I decided to put my mother to the test.

It was now about six months after Martin's death, and I had disposed of all his clothes. However, I was able to buy a suit identical to the one he was wearing when he died. The next time my mother visited me I showed it to her, asking "do you recognise this?" "Oh yes," she replied, "that's what Martin was wearing in my vision, but it was paler than the one in your hand." She was correct, for Martin's suit had faded through washing.

My mother's vision was clearly intended to comfort us and relieve our suffering, and became even more precious to me as the months passed.

Later on, with some other people, I helped to found a research unit to investigate the cot death syndrome. I do not feel that I could have undertaken this without the spiritual help I received after the loss of my own baby.'

★★*★*★

'My father died when I was five years old. My brother and I were told by our nanny how devoted he was to us.

Some 30 years later I had a strange experience. I was in hospital after a minor operation. I lay in bed worrying about the outcome of this when suddenly I saw my father standing by my bed. I recognised him instantly, with his serious square face, square shoulders and penetrating blue eyes. He was telling me "It will be alright".

I have no doubt whatsoever about his presence there – and everything was indeed alright. I have since thought with gratitude how after all these years my father is still watching over me.'

★★*★*★

'I'd come into the house after working in the garden one summer evening. I was a little tired, and sat down in my chair in the study with my dog beside me. It was about a year since the death of my wife, and I missed her all the time. I slept for a while and then awoke.

Suddenly I saw my wife standing smiling in front of me – just as she used to look before her dreadful illness. "Oh hello", I said, thinking for a moment that she'd come to tell me dinner was ready; then she vanished – and I was fully back in the present, alone. Nothing like this had ever happened before. I was immensely comforted and quite certain that I did not imagine the event. My eyes were wide open when I saw her.'

★★★★★★★★

'The following experience occurred about five months after my husband's death. I was in bed reading one day when I looked up and saw my husband smiling warmly and holding out his hand to me; he was dressed in clothes which I recognised. He was standing above me as if in a rectangular picture frame, and I saw down to his knees. Behind him was bright sunshine and greenery, and he looked so well, and only about 45 – the age at which he married me. He was in the prime of life – although he had been an elderly man when he died. A radiance shone from him. The vision lasted briefly, then was gone; if only I'd been able to prolong it.'

★★★★★★★★

'During the Second World War I worked for the Red Cross, and delivered books to the hospitals for them. One day I went to the Richmond Hospital for artificial limbs. At the end of the ward I noticed screens surrounding a bed, and asked a nurse if I should offer the patient a book. "He might like one" she replied, "but he's very ill – both legs have gone."

As I approached the patient he greeted me, "Hello Lady Newall, I'm so glad to see you; I met you in Cairo when I was serving there." He'd been in one of the regiments of Footguards, and was entertained by my husband and myself. I talked to him, giving all

93

the encouragement I could, and then departed. Not long afterwards I learned that he had died.

Some time later I went to my club, the Ladies' Carlton, at Hyde Park Corner. There was a queue of people waiting to see the hall porter near the entrance, and I noticed amongst them a pale distressed young woman who was limping. Something made me look up to the right hand top transom of the long Georgian window. Clearly framed in its half circle I saw the head and shoulders of the young man I'd visited in hospital. His face was alive, and his lips moved; "Help her", he said, "Help her . . ." I knew at once to whom he was referring. Spontaneously I turned to the pale young woman and asked if I could be of any assistance. It transpired that she had been bombed out the previous night, and had hurt her foot on some sharp gravel. She was desperately trying to find accommodation, but as she was not a member of the club I had to tell her that unfortunately there was no hope for her there.

I then offered her a room temporarily in my country house, and shortly afterwards we drove there and she stayed for nearly a month. My husband made no objection for he well knew that I was not subject to hallucinations or imaginative day-dreams, and we both felt deeply moved by the vision's message of survival.

At first the young woman said little about herself, then one day she told me that she had come from South Africa in order to marry the officer whom I'd visited in hospital. She had reached him just before he died. I described my vision in the hope of comforting her.

The episode has an interesting sequel. Later on the young woman returned to South Africa and eventually married. Years passed by and then her daughter came to live in Gloucestershire, near our home in Badminton. We met, quite by chance, and she told me that her mother had related to her the tremendous help she'd received from me during the war owing to a wonderful and timely vision.'

★★★★★★★★

'In my dream we were in the sitting room at home. I was at one end of it, and opposite was the familiar Welsh dresser covered with

94

pewter mugs. I was standing in the room, and felt my father, who had died sometime previously, standing behind me. We started talking, and his attitude towards me was quite different from what it used to be. I remember thinking "this is wonderful – why couldn't our relationship have been like this during his lifetime?" (We were never really on the same wavelength.) Now he was unbelievably nice to me! Then I realised that he'd moved something in the room. It was characteristic of his liking for order (he used to mutter "why can't things ever be put back in their proper place!"). As I awoke I had a totally different impression of my father's feelings for me – and now I'm actually looking forward to seeing him again one day!'

★★★★★★★★

'In July 1944, having fought at Salerno, I was in Rome awaiting another appointment, when I received a telephone call from my Commanding Officer. He suggested meeting for lunch. As soon as we sat down he said "I've got sad news for you, I'm afraid. Bill has been killed". This was shatering news. Bill had been one of my best friends since Oxford days and I was his child's godfather. I had been responsible for encouraging him to join the Scots Guards at the outbreak of the Second World War.

After lunch I went disconsolately out into the July sunshine and walked until I found a church. It was charming, very small and dark, and empty. I went up to the front pew and knelt to pray for Bill and his family, whom I knew and loved. I was torn by my grief as I prayed. But suddenly I felt marvellous, and the next moment I was outside my body, standing up. I turned round and there, in a blaze of light, was Bill, a few yards away and a few feet above the floor level. He was with several others whom I could not see clearly enough to recognise. I saw Bill *very* clearly, and he looked at me with the most wonderful smile. I knew he was telling me that all was very well.

The vision faded, I was back in my body, and I left the church, light of heart and step. The euphoria did not last very long, but I knew I had seen a miracle and I have cherished the memory ever since.'

★★★★★★★

'I used not to believe in an afterlife, but one night I had a remarkable dream which convinced me that another unseen world does exist.

My father, mother and step-mother had all been dead for some time. My sister Jane, and her fiancé, Peter, were abroad. I'd always had a special relationship with my sister and had tried to help and protect her. But now I was worried about her, wondering if I'd been right in encouraging her to marry Peter – I wasn't sure how the family would have accepted him, had they lived. My reassurance came in the most wonderful way, through an astonishingly vivid dream. My father, with whom I shared a strong rapport, came to me saying "I want you to know how terribly happy we all are, and how much we like Peter. And we want to thank you for everything you've done for Jane – you've always looked after her." It was exactly as if Daddy was physically present, talking to me.

As I awoke I wished so much that I could have spent a longer time with him . . . I cried as I told my husband about it during the morning. The wonderful experience was over all too quickly.

When my sister returned from abroad I asked her if by any chance she had dreamed of the family. She was surprised, but answered, "Yes, as a matter of fact I dreamed of Daddy. He was glowing with happiness for Peter and I." '

★★★★★★★

'I was suffering the misery of loneliness after my husband's death, and in my dream I was carrying a chair – plodding slowly up a hill in my village and feeling that on no account must I put it down.

My husband and I loved this low-slung oak chair which he had given to me. It was very heavy, but some impulse made me struggle on. Suddenly I put the chair down heavily with the thought "I can't carry this burden any further!" "Oh yes you can, I know you can," I heard Simon say distinctly. This time when I lifted the chair it was so light that I managed quite easily. The surprise and shock of its lightness woke me with a start, and I immediately realised the poignant significance of my dream. The burden of loneliness without Simon had seemed unbearable – but never again did I feel such despair.'

★★★★★★★★

'I was terribly worried, because all contact with a deeply loved friend, a regular correspondent, had suddenly ceased. All I could do was to pray.

One evening when I was washing up, I distinctly heard my dead husband's voice behind me saying "Peggy's much better – don't worry." I was so shaken at hearing my husband's voice that I dropped a plate!

I decided to write at once to Peggy, and put the letter in the hall ready for the post. However, to my astonishment the very next morning I received a letter from her! She explained that as a result of being knocked down by a car, she had been in a nursing home for a year (she was without family). She had lost her memory, and suffered much, but was better now. She hadn't realised the length of time since our last correspondence, "but last night" she wrote, "you seemed to be talking to me – you were so close."

It was the answer to my prayer. My letter was still in the hall, and Peggy's letter was written the day before my husband spoke to me. I was so happy, and deeply moved by my husband's understanding of my state, and the situation I was in.'

★★★★★★★★

'I was lying awake in bed one night when I clearly heard my name called by my dead brother. There was no mistaking my brother's voice for he used to pronounce my name in a particular way. Then I felt him grip my hand – and I knew my brother's grip! He had an extremely strong grip as a result of much training and exercise. He told me "I'm alright", and gripped my hand again.

Suddenly I realised that it was eight years ago to the day that he'd died of tuberculosis. He'd come to me on the anniversary of his death, and at the exact hour – 1.00 a.m. We were very close, my brother and I – tremendous friends. I must admit that until this amazing experience I had not given much thought to an afterlife.'

****

'My daughter-in-law, Catherine, told me the following story about her 80-year-old mother, who had been ill for some time. She and her mother had always been very close.

Catherine was awakened in the middle of the night by a beautiful smell of violets, the scent she always associated with her mother, and the feeling of someone gently stroking her hair, exactly as her mother used to do in childhood when she came to say goodnight. Catherine turned on the light, but saw nobody. Her husband awoke and asked what was the matter. She told him, then, baffled, they fell asleep again.

The following morning they learned that Catherine's mother had died in the night.'

****

'My mother and father, recently married, were sitting chatting in the drawing room at the time of this incident. My father's youngest brother, Bobby, aged 19 at the time, was chaplain to an Officers' Training Corps in the north of England. He always wore Harris tweed jackets, and when they were wet they produced a distinct smell! The family used to tease him about this.

On the day in question, at 2.30 p.m., my mother suddenly noticed that there was a strong smell of Harris tweed. "Bobby must have arrived" she said, and went to look over the banisters, calling

"Come upstairs". No reply. Later my parents received a telegram informing them that there had been a tragic accident; Bobby had been shot and killed by what was supposed to have been a blank cartridge – at exactly 2.30 p.m.'

★★★★★★★★

'For a couple of months before he died, my husband became particularly trying – rather like a spoilt child – and he was at his most difficult in the evenings. I wondered if he could be unwell, although there was nothing to suggest this. The doctor gave him a thorough examination, and my husband, Bill, was delighted when he was pronounced very fit for his age.

One evening we were in the midst of a heated argument. I was about to retaliate when suddenly I heard a voice (and I actually turned round to see who had intervened) saying "Stop it – it won't be long." Instantly I understood the meaning, and obeyed the voice.

Bill died of an embolism on the lung just a week later and I was with him at the time.

Two strange and wonderful events followed his death. On one occasion I was sitting alone in a very depressed state with the dogs on my lap, when I felt my husband conveying to me "You're not to worry – I didn't look after you on earth, but I'm doing so now." Again, when I was anxious about my house, I heard his comforting words "You'll sell the house next month." To my intense relief I did.

Since these incidents I've occasionally become aware of my husband's presence, and look forward with confidence and joy to meeting him again one day.'

CHAPTER VI

Shafts of Light

by

The Revd F. M. Drake

FOR MOST OF US, I BELIEVE, the direction taken by our lives is controlled, for good or ill, by the influence of parents, teachers and friends, by our reading, and to some extent by heredity and environment. But in my own life I have occasionally been granted shafts of light from the unseen, bringing me guidance and help when these were especially necessary, and I know that many others have had the same experience. Moreover many older folk will agree, as they look back, that there has been an ordained pattern in their lives, which led them to develop stage by stage: a process to which we are all subject, but which we disturb or delay by our wrong choices. As an older man I have come to realise that this pattern is controlled by the action of that divine love to which we are all linked, from which we emerged, and to which, I believe, we shall eventually return. I wholly subscribe to Carolyn's choice of *Love, the Eternal Link* as the title for this book.

Though many of us at one time or another receive these shafts of light, frequently we do not recognise their significance. Personally, and for my own convenience, I divide them roughly into two categories, the psychic and the spiritual, but these are really different aspects of the same phenomenon and frequently overlap. I must stress that I have no authority for this division.

For me the former, that is the psychic, consists of clairvoyance, clairaudience, precognition and similar extrasensory perceptions, which appear to be latent in every human mind. They are not necessarily dependent upon the prayer, or the prayer-life, of the individual. The spiritual experiences however, do arise necessarily from prayer or the prayer-life.

An experience which might be regarded as either psychic or spiritual is the following. During the last war my wife and I booked a room at the Francis Hotel in Bath in order to visit relatives in the town. On arrival we found that the town had been extensively bombed during the night. Having picked our way through streets covered in broken glass and water spilled from fire-hoses, we were sitting at supper in the hotel when my wife suddenly announced her conviction that a second bombing raid would occur that night. Neither she nor I were accustomed to receiving premonitions, and I protested, because at that time the Germans, though bombing a number of small towns each night, were not in the habit of bombing the same town twice running. They preferred to spread their fire, and Bath was now probably the safest small town in England. My wife won. We spent the night outside Bath, and returned the next day to find that the town had indeed been bombed a second time, and that the Francis Hotel had virtually disappeared, and had been replaced by the biggest conical pile of bricks we had ever seen. My wife burst into tears.

Many lives were lost under that pile of bricks. Had she for the first time in her life received a warning, sent because our lives would be needed for some purpose later on?

★★★★★★★★

I am convinced that God has an over-all plan for every human life. In the following pages I will try to show how, through a progressive series of spiritual experiences, I was shown what I believe to have been His plan for my own life.

In my early thirties an event occurred which was to influence me permanently. At this time, in spite of the great job satisfaction which I was enjoying as a housemaster in one of our smaller public schools, my inner life was causing me deep unrest. I prayed for help. The help was given in the following manner.

101

Quite unexpectedly, a friend with whom I had been a fellow undergraduate at Oxford came to visit me. I was astonished at the change in him. His carriage was erect, his eyes shone with enthusiasm, he was bursting with vitality. When I asked him if there was any special reason for his visit, he told me that he had committed his life to God, and was eager for me to do the same! I was impressed but extremely cautious.

Shortly after this I visited him at Eastbourne. We were sitting on the front enjoying the mild spring sunshine. My eyes were momentarily shut and suddenly I saw, in spite of my closed eyes, a banner, or scroll, on which were written with great distinctness the words "Put less trust in yourself and more in Me." This was the first of four commands which I was to receive from the unseen.

I was deeply moved, and after much prayer and thought decided to make an experiment, to do some research as it were.

The Experiment

For exactly three weeks, no more, no less, I would live so far as was practically possible as if Jesus Christ was alive in the flesh, and I His companion and disciple, guided and controlled by Him. I would treat His teachings and the four Gospels as representing, for me, ultimate truth. I worked very hard at this but told no one. In order to concentrate my mind on the idea that He was my constant companion, I even opened doors for Him to precede me as I went from room to room, and opened gates for Him when I went on country walks. After three weeks the result was astonishing. My whole outlook had changed, and my life now had purpose and direction, together with the conviction that Jesus Christ was still alive, and was indeed for me the Way, the Truth and the Life.

This was followed by two contacts with the unseen. The first occurred one morning when I had gone down to the masters' common room to collect my letters from the tier of pigeon holes where one of the office staff used to put them each morning. As I stood there for a moment with the letters in my hand, a message was projected . . . I can use no other word . . . into my mind. It was wholly unexpected and not altogether welcome. "If you don't take Holy Orders, your life will have failed of its purpose". This was the second of the four commands. The words were curt and allowed of no argument. And, ever since I have known that it is in fact possible to receive a call from God, to have a 'vocation' in the strict sense of that word. And in due course I did in fact take Holy Orders and became a clergyman according to the Anglican rite.

It was no doubt my willingness to obey this command that brought about in natural sequence a further contact with the unseen. Late one night, not long before midnight, I was walking home from school, where I had spent some time talking with the headmaster. My way lay across a playing field, then through a gap in the hedge into a lane and thence, after some 70 yards, on to the main London road. When I was some little way across the field I suddenly became afraid: afraid for my family, my friends, and for my own future. Fear gripped me. I prayed, crossed myself repeatedly, but kept on walking, thanking God that the fear was gradually relaxing its grip.

When finally I slipped through the gap in the hedge into the lane I was joined by two invisible 'persons' who accompanied me as I walked, one on my left and one on my right. Though they were invisible I was acutely aware of their presence. Several times I looked right and left, wanting to speak to them, but somehow feeling that it would be wrong to do so.

I have to confess that throughout my life I had suffered from vague fears and apprehensions. And now my two companions began, literally, to inject me with a strong quality of fearlessness. There was no question about it. I could feel the thing happening. As I walked down the darkened lane, tall bushes on one side of me, an open field on the other, I was conscious of a new freedom from fear, and the knowledge that nothing evil could have any lasting power over me. I remember comparing myself, as the feeling grew and grew, to a small ship between two larger ones being refuelled by them, through a pipe across the water.

103

As I left the lane and entered the main London road, my companions left me, and in my strong and joyful exultation I fell to measuring this new state of fearlessness. If a bull were now to come thundering down the road towards me, intent on destroying me, yes, I would certainly jump over that fence by the side of the road, but, wonder of wonders, I would not be in the least afraid. And if a German tank loaded with death-dealing young Nazis, for this was in the late 1930s, were to come racing towards me, why of course I would leap for cover but I would not be afraid. All fear had left me.

This experience was sent to me, I am sure, as a kind of introduction to the new life which I had been commanded to lead. In any event it came as a shaft of light, reminding me of the link of love that exists between ourselves and a loving God, and proving to me that we are watched over and strengthened by guardian angels.

After the war, which I spent as chaplain and housemaster at a public school in the Midlands, I went out to India with my wife and younger son, Nicholas, to take over the headmastership of an English public school for English and Indian boys. Perched among deodar forests 7,000 feet above the sea, the school buildings looked out southwards towards the wide plains of India, and northwards towards the snowcapped peaks of the high Himalayan ranges. It was a place of enchanting, breath-taking beauty.

Splendidly equipped in spite of its geographical position, the school had everything; up-to-date science laboratories, a good library, a fine chapel, swimming pool, gymnasium, facilities for cricket, hockey and football; and an excellent climate. But after our first two years the political thunderstorm that had long been threatening finally exploded. The partition of India under Lord Mountbatten, the departure of the British, the murder of Mahatma Gandhi, the hundreds of thousands of murders that were committed in the Punjab, all combined to maintain a dark climate of uncertainty, distrust and fear. Fortunately for us in our mountain fastness, the effect of these disasters, though considerable, was indirect rather than direct.

It so happened that when the time came for me to take my family back to Europe, in December, on three months leave, my wife had recently contracted an undiagnosed illness, and my first task in London was to take her to the Hospital for Tropical Diseases. Here she was told that if she returned to India her health would be gravely at risk.

It was therefore with a heavy heart that I decided that in March I should have to return alone to an India that was no longer under British rule.

We returned from London to the home of my wife's parents in Guernsey and, once there, a profound depression descended upon me; a dark forecast of what lay ahead; perhaps a form of precognition. This depression lasted for the greater part of my three months' leave. It was with me all day, accompanied me to bed, and was waiting for me as I awoke. And then, when all the travel arrangements for my return to India had been made, and my tickets bought and paid for, I awoke one morning to find that the depression had suddenly disappeared. It was dramatic. The world was once again a lovely place and it was good to be alive. Then came the clear knowledge that I must take my Bible, pencil and paper and go and spend an hour or two on the nearby cliffs which overlooked the sea. For a while I sat quietly in the sun, reading and resting. And then, suddenly, I received the third of the four commands, short and crystal clear, injected into my mind. "You must go back to India." But of course, I thought, everything is arranged. My passage is booked, my tickets paid for. It seemed quite pointless, even silly. Nonetheless, feeling rather foolish, I wrote the message down. After a pause, a second message came. "You must trust me more than ever before." This was the fourth command. This too I wrote down. Then came a third and final message. "It will be all right." What, I wondered, would be 'all right'?

The rest of that day was clear and happy, and that night I slept deeply. But next morning I received a letter from the Chairman of my Board of Governors, who also was on leave in Europe, requiring an immediate reply and enclosing a second letter which he himself had just received from India. This was a document signed by a senior member of my staff, and countersigned by a senior member of the ministry of education for that part of India, demanding my removal from the office of headmaster for embezzlement, incompetence, drunkenness and much else. It was a formidable attack, planned to be effective when both I and the Chairman were away from India. The fact that the charges were untrue did nothing to comfort me, nor did it occur to me that a member of my staff could possibly be trying to get my job for himself, as later was to become abundantly clear. This attack threatened a shame and humiliation (for the school at that time was one of the most well-known throughout the sub-continent of India) that must surely haunt me for the rest of my days.

My depression at once returned. And to my shame I have to admit that my first and immediate reaction was "I won't go back. I won't go back to India." And then I remembered. The message "You must go back" which I had received the day before and which had seemed so pointless at the time, now struck me with its full force and meaning. So, I returned to India, to defend my case and carry on with my job, trusting wholly in God as I had been told to do. But my return had been essential, for my non-appearance would have indicated either cowardice or an admission of guilt. As it was, the case was fully examined, I was fully exonerated and the Governors wrote me a letter which I shall treasure for the rest of my life.

Six little words, written down on a slip of paper, had saved me. Someone in the unseen had foreseen it all and warned me in advance. For many years I kept that slip of paper, until finally it became indecipherable.

It is important to remember that the link of love can be made more operative, and spiritual perception stimulated, by prayer and concentration.

Not long after our return from India, our elder son Robin, aged 24, contracted Hodgkin's disease, a cancerous illness which at that time was considered fatal. When, after two spells at Guy's Hospital, it finally became clear that medical science could not cure the disease, Robin, my wife and I devoted ourselves to prayer, and with all the determination at our command concentrated upon achieving as Christian and prayerful a way of living and thinking as lay within

106

our power. We introduced this period, which in the event was to last for two years, with a solemn ceremony, in which Robin committed himself and his entire future, both in this world and the next, to Almighty God, and sealed this act of self-surrender by receiving the Sacrament of Holy Unction.

Throughout these two years, and at every available moment (for my wife and I were now fully occupied with the school which we were running in my old home) my mind was continuously concentrated upon the love, the presence and the power of God, and into these three I repeatedly brought my son Robin. There was nothing pious or churchy about this concentration. I was just a simple middle-aged man, desperately anxious for the health of his son.

My wife and Robin, each in their own way, were praying also. But Robin was far more spiritually minded than either of his parents.

It was, I am sure, as a direct result of this two-year session of prayer, directed really towards one single purpose, that an inter-related sequence of events was now able to occur, one following another in natural order, each a link in a chain of love, linking us with the unseen.

First (it was now mid-winter), in the lane behind the spot where the Chapel of Christ the Healer now stands, I was once again lifting my heart to God in fervent prayer when instantly my prayers were answered, though in a way I could never have expected. For a few unforgettable moments I actually saw, with ocular vision, that all created things round me were alive, alive with the life of God. Everything within reach of my sight, from the nearest twig to the most distant cloud above the far horizon of the sea, suddenly became brand new, just as if it had, at that moment, emerged from the hands of the Creator. Everything, I repeat everything, was alive, happy, shining inwardly, and apparently conscious. I was able unhurriedly to examine each leaf or plant and contemplate their celestial appearance. This was an aspect of eternal life which was quite new to me.

Then, my whole personality, body, mind and spirit, was invaded by something which could be felt. I was surrounded and shaken by some power which grasped me, held me, and reduced me in that same instant to tears . . . a voice, deep within me, said "Thy son liveth", and I was conscious, as I believed then and believe now, of the near presence of Our Lord Himself. With deep conviction I concluded that God meant to give Robin back his physical life here on earth. He had intervened, and our son would live. But the real meaning of the words 'Thy son liveth' was not to be made plain until after Robin's death.

Soon after this the clear knowledge was given to my wife Joanna, through her prayers, that Robin must go to the late Miss Dorothy Kerin's Home of Healing at Burrswood, in Kent. This visit was to have far-reaching results.

Following this I received a vivid mental vision of a miniature church, with a square tower, standing in what was then the rather disreputable chicken run at the back of the old farm house which was our home. Six months later the vision returned with such vividness that I felt compelled to have rough plans drafted by an architect. Having no money, however, with which to erect such a building, I put the plan away in a drawer.

When Robin returned from Burrswood, Miss Kerin, now well known as one of the most remarkable and gifted Christian visionaries of our time, came with him and insisted that it was God's will that a chapel should be built, without delay, upon that spot. When I protested, "Do you mean that I am to give an order to a contractor now, without having the money with which to pay him?", she replied, "Of course I do. God has the money. What you have to do is to get started immediately, without a moment's delay. Do it now".

Within 24 hours, though a stranger to the island, she had found an anonymous donor who would pay all expenses. Work began at once, and the completed chapel was dedicated, by the then Bishop of our Diocese of Winchester, to Christ the Healer. The correctness of Miss Kerin's belief that the building of the chapel was God's will is indicated by the many blessings and healings which have followed prayer there. It is worthy of note that none of this could have happened if Joanna had not obeyed her clear guidance that Robin must go to Burrswood.

Dorothy's visits to Guernsey, and later to our chapel, were to make an enormous impact upon Robin, Joanna and myself, for her entire life was governed by one implacable conviction, that her Master and Lord, Jesus Christ, is alive today, yesterday and for ever. She claimed to have seen Him on a number of occasions, and many times to have heard, and been able to recognise, His voice. I believe her. Later, as her chaplain at Burrswood for two years, I learned to appreciate her great spiritual gifts, her intellectual integrity and her sound Irish common sense. Her relationship with God was above all a strictly personal one, and so great was her devotion to her Lord that she would certainly have accepted crucifixion if that had been necessary. In no other life in modern times, I am sure, has the link of love been more clearly manifested.

From babyhood her deeply religious nature had been evident. As she herself wrote later: 'Especially I have to thank God for vouchsafing me a feeling of His presence ever with me, which I have had ever since I can remember anything'.

But Robin's health did not improve. In spite of some remission it grew steadily worse, until at last he became an exceedingly sick man, terribly weak, in constant pain, his limbs just plain bones covered by a thin covering of skin.

For some strange reason we never believed that he was dying, confident, as he was, that Our Lord would still heal him. We held a service of re-dedication, and for the second time he received Holy Unction. I think I can say with humility that our faith in prayer did not waver.

Then, within some 24 hours, he was miraculously invaded by great spiritual vitality. He became effortlessly carefree, and filled more and more with love and peace and joy, each of those great qualities separately recognisable and never to leave him until the moment of his death.

Robin died, very quietly, one night at about 3.00 a.m. When, next morning, I telephoned the news to Dorothy Kerin, she told me that at 3.00 a.m. she had been woken by a hand roughly shaking her by the shoulder, and Robin's voice saying loudly and joyfully, "Muzz" (her nickname), "I'm all right now."

That evening Joanna and I and a close friend were puzzling about what words to use as a heading on the funeral leaflet. 'Entered into Rest' seemed inappropriate for a young man of only 28. Suddenly the telephone rang. Once again it was Dorothy Kerin, more than a hundred miles away. She sounded shy and embarrassed, for she could have no idea what Joanna and I were doing at that moment, and what she had to say might seem pointless.

"Frank," she said, "I hope you won't think I'm mad, but I have an urgent message for you, to be delivered immediately. The words you want are these: 'For so He giveth his beloved sleep' (we realised later that these words were an extract from Psalm 27). Now does that make sense?" And she added, "It was Robin's voice that spoke to me."

So Our Lord had not broken his promise, for Robin was alive and well in the world of spirit. Indeed, His promise 'Thy son Liveth' was abundantly true.

His death was immediately followed, at least so far as I was concerned, by a remarkable phenomenon. It seemed that everything around us, house, chapel, garden, was full of joy. I could only suppose that this was Robin's own joy, his delight in his new surroundings spilling over into our own. During the two days before the funeral I realised that I must conduct it myself, and also give the address. This I did: receiving the necessary strength to go right through the service before being overcome by emotion. An extract from the address reads as follows:–

'Never once in several years, even at the worst moments, did we hear him complain. On the contrary, he dedicated himself to Christ's service, and if only by his unfailing consideration for human beings, he showed his unfailing love for God. He said often

110

"through this illness I am getting a training that can be got in no other way".

And the training was successful. About six weeks before he died, Our Lord touched him with the gifts of the Holy Spirit, and he became radiant with peace, and love and joy. Often he said how close Our Lord was to him. It is absolutely true to say that the more ill and miserable he became physically, the more cause he found to praise God. This is the authentic sign of God's divine healing. Until the day of his death he expected to be healed, so that he might serve Christ in this world. But Christ did not heal him . . . physically. Robin died.

This is not defeat, but victory. Physically, the disease defeated him. Spiritually and morally, he defeated it, being through Christ more than conqueror. His training is complete. Honestly I believe that already in the next world he is serving the Master whom he would have served in this.'

But Robin did not leave us immediately. Indeed, on various occasions I knew that he was close beside me. For instance, a few weeks later I was asked to visit a very elderly lady, a great-aunt of Robin's, who was ill in bed, had very little faith and was frightened. I did not relish the idea of going. Suddenly I became aware, with absolute conviction, and as though it were the most natural thing in the world, that Robin would accompany me. This, very evidently, he did. The difficult visit turned out to be entirely smooth and easy, and was very successful.

Six weeks after his death Joanna and I visited Burrswood as the personal guests of Miss Kerin; she and Robin had been very close, and she had treated him as if he were an adopted son.

He had previously given her a beautiful silver rose-bowl, and the first thing we noticed, as Dorothy showed us into our bedroom, was this rose-bowl, filled with the most gorgeous roses. When I exclaimed with delight, she simply said "Oh, that wasn't my idea. It was Robin who suggested it."

To quote from my book *Thy son Liveth*: 'Robin has been with us many times since he left us on Wednesday, October 23rd 1957. He

111

has been more often, we think, to Burrswood, busy in the ministry of healing. Whenever he is near, I am aware of a spirit of great power and stature, pure, bright and strong. Praise be to God.'

★★★★★★★★

In the life of Dorothy Kerin, as in the lives of other saints (for I consider her to be a saint), strange and inexplicable things used sometimes to happen, not merely spectacular healings of the incurably sick, but little, seemingly unimportant happenings. No doubt such folk live so close to God that in their case the veil that separates our world from the next has become thinner?

On one occasion, for instance, my wife and I had given up our bedroom for Dorothy, who was staying some days with us. On one of the walls there was a crucifix and below it a reproduction of a well-known painting of Jesus Christ, head only, as He may have looked. Undoubtedly Dorothy must have spent some time looking at them both, as she lay in bed.

After Dorothy's departure Joanna and I moved back into our room. A few days later, at about 5.00 a.m., Joanna woke me and said, "Look at that." The picture, glowing with a rosy light, was somehow 'lit up' from within, so that it seemed to be giving out light, rather than being illuminated by exterior light. She told me that, before she woke me, the crucifix had also been bathed in its own light. The picture was still glowing when we returned to sleep some five minutes later.

I spent a considerable time trying to satisfy myself that this strange light could be attributed to natural causes. But it was quite useless. In the end I had to admit that it came from a supernatural, or at least from a humanly inexplicable, source.

I would like to end this appendix with an account of two occasions, both due to Dorothy's influence, direct or indirect, in which Christ demonstrated His presence at a Service of Holy Communion. The first concerned the bread (hereafter referred to as the wafer), the second concerned the wine.

During my chaplaincy at Burrswood, Dorothy told me of her wish to have the Sacrament 'reserved' in the chapel there. This may need some explanation.

The rules of the Church require that all wafers and wine consecrated at a communion service must be consumed by the clergy and congregation during or immediately after the service. In certain cases, however, the Bishop may give permission for the priest, at regular intervals, to retain a small number of the consecrated wafers, each intincted at the centre with a minute drop of consecrated wine, and to 'reserve' them in a locked ambry in his church or chapel. They are thus ready and available to be taken to any dying person, or to one too sick to attend even a shortened form of the communion service. It should be added that Christians believe that the wafers and wine, once consecrated, become through the power of the Holy Spirit – in a strictly heavenly and spiritual sense – a vehicle for Christ's presence and action in the lives of those who consume them.

I obtained the necessary permission on Dorothy's behalf but this had never been implemented: largely, I think, because of Dorothy's forthcoming tour in America.

Dorothy was much exhausted by this tour, and on her return my wife and I and certain members of the staff, being concerned for her health, prayed together on her behalf to Our Lord, whose special protegé we believed her to be. This was on a Monday evening.

These prayers were to be answered in a most unusual way.

During that Monday night, Dorothy received a vision of Our Lord, in which He said to her "Dorothy, I am going to come and dwell in Burrswood in quite a new way." She told no one about this vision.

The following morning, Tuesday, was the weekday on which Dorothy and I, after the congregation in the chapel had received Holy Communion, always took the wafers and wine to the bedrooms of those who were too sick to come downstairs. On this occasion there were 19 communicants in the chapel, and 10 sick folk to be visited in their bedrooms. With Dorothy and myself this amounted to 31 persons in all, but in fact I consecrated 32 wafers, in case there should be a latecomer to the chapel.

I should mention that the counting of heads, before consecration took place, was invariably done with the greatest care and accuracy.

This was Dorothy's chapel, and she was a perfectionist, especially in all matters concerning her beloved Lord.

When all was finished and the last bedroom visited, there remained of course only one wafer. I covered the chalice and paten, that is, the cup and the plate, and we returned to the chapel, where I prepared to remove the linen coverings and to consume the remaining wafer. Dorothy, as always, was standing by my side. No one else was within 10 yards of us. As I uncovered the paten, we found ourselves confronted, not by one wafer, but by a small pile.

Neither of us could speak. For a very long moment we remained tongue-tied, but finally I said "Does this mean that Our Lord has chosen this occasion as the one on which we are to reserve the Sacrament?" She didn't answer me for a moment, but then she said, "I'll go and get the pyx", that is, the little silver container in which the Sacrament can be reserved. It took her fully 10 minutes to go to her own house at the far end of Burrswood, find the pyx, and return to the chapel. When at last she reached the porch at the lower end of the chapel and walked up the aisle, she was repeating to herself in a whisper that was plainly audible, "It's a miracle. It's a great miracle." And at the altar she used the same words to me.

It was only after we had reserved the Sacrament and returned to the vestry that she said, "Now Frank, I'll tell you why it is such a great miracle. Last night, in the very middle of the night, Our Lord came and stood in the doorway of my room. And He said, 'Dorothy, I am going to come and dwell in Burrswood in quite a new way.'" She then went on to say that it had been a physical appearance, insisting that His form appeared to be material and solid.

I must stress once again that Dorothy and I were working in the closest conjunction when this remarkable thing happened. She had been beside me, watching me, as, early in the service, I counted out the wafers on to the paten. She was standing close beside me, right by my side, watching, as she always did, when I finally uncovered the paten, to discover that one wafer had been multiplied into a little pile. And it is important to note that at the time when this event took place, Dorothy did not know that some of us had been praying for her on the previous evening nor did I, for my part, know that Our Lord had visited her a few hours later.

What was the purpose of this miracle?

Primarily, one must assume, to indicate Our Lord's wish that the Sacrament should be reserved at Burrswood, at least during Dorothy's lifetime; but by no means necessarily in every other church or chapel.

But there is, I think, a further purpose. Some years ago I heard an Anglican clergyman, in the pulpit, explain away Our Lord's miracle of the Feeding of the Five Thousand. Our Lord, he said, was so full of grace that his hearers were charmed into producing the food which they had concealed about their persons, and into sharing it with others. This of course may have happened. Yet with all my heart I believe that Our Lord did indeed multiply the loaves and fishes, exactly as all four Gospels say that he did . . . and exactly as He multiplied that one wafer at Burrswood.

I believe that on this occasion Our Lord simply speeded up, by His touch, the great law of multiplication, which the Creator has ordained in one form or another throughout the universe. Each little acorn (Dorothy's personal symbol was an acorn) potentially contains within itself a multitude, a whole forest, of giant oak trees; and this in itself, if we could but grasp the fact, is miraculous. Under Our Lord's touch this great law of increase, to which in its normal and unhurried form we human beings are accustomed, can be expanded and speeded up. To this speeding-up we are not accustomed, and we think of it, quite reasonably, as miraculous.

If only, therefore, as a perpetual reminder that today, as then, He can, with very little to work on, still feed His disciples, both spiritually and physically, this miracle at Burrswood had its purpose.

The second occasion on which I was shown Our Lord's presence at the Communion Service came about like this.

In the centre, and at the back, of the altar in our Chapel of Christ the Healer in Guernsey there is a wooden cross, standing some 18 inches high. During Communion Services a silver cup, containing the wine about to be consecrated, used to stand in front of this cross, and some way away from it. A peculiarity of this particular early Victorian cup is that its outer surface is not smooth but incrusted with little silver protuberances which stand out about a quarter of an inch. During the services, at the time of which I am writing, the cup used to be kept covered with a lace cloth. A most unwise arrangement, as I was to discover.

One morning, standing before the altar and about to administer the cup, with its now consecrated wine, to kneeling members of the congregation, I used less than my usual care in lifting the lace cloth from its upper surface. As I did so, a corner of the lace became caught on an incrustation at the back of the cup, and the cup, inevitably pulled towards me, tipped forwards and spilled its contents on to the main altar cloth. None of the wine, obviously, was spilled backwards towards the cross.

Deeply shocked, as every priest will understand, that my lack of care should have resulted in the violation of such a sacred moment, I fell spontaneously to my knees and poured out to God my sorrow at what I had done. When I opened my eyes, the first thing they fell upon was the cross . . . standing at the back of the altar and well behind the spilled wine . . . and on it, some six or eight inches above the surface of the altar, I saw a drop of dark red blood, clinging to one of the curves on the upgoing stem of the cross. As I gazed at it, I had not the slightest doubt that it was, in fact, blood, for unlike wine, it was thick and consistent.

To the sceptics I would reply:– "That is not the end of the matter. For how on earth could a single individual drop of wine, defying all the laws of gravity, separating itself without so much as a smear from the parent body of the out-spilled wine, find its lonely way up on to the cross? For it was, in fact alone. There was no trace even of moisture, either on the cross or away from the circle of spilled wine."

I have used the phrase 'How on earth . . .' but was I, at that moment entirely 'on earth'? I have long suspected that sometimes, when we are most deeply involved in prayer, that part of us with which we pray enters a higher dimension and momentarily we may be shown, in visible terms, that which is not normally visible to us because it belongs to a higher dimension.

Finally we must repeat our belief that, in every human life, little (yet not always so little) recognisable contacts with the unseen do occur, such as we have tried to illustrate; and we know them to be important, for they stimulate our remembrance and vision of the unseen. The psalmist goes further and tells us 'Where there is no vision, the people perish.'

Our English poets, who see so very much deeper than most of us can ever hope to, have much to say on this subject. Francis Thompson in his poem *The Kingdom of God* reminds us :–

'O world invisible, we view thee,
O world intangible, we touch thee,
O world unknowable, we know thee,
Inapprehensible, we clutch thee.'

And in a later verse he reminds us how even the moss beneath a stone, or a brightly coloured insect, can be a message . . . or messenger, for we have seen that angel really means messenger ! . . . of the link of love between God and his creation.

'The angels keep their ancient places ;–
Turn but a stone, and start a wing !
'Tis ye, 'tis your estranged faces,
That miss the many-splendoured thing.'

We pray for you, who have read these lines, that Our Father in heaven will grant you such shafts of light as may illumine for you the link of love that binds you to him.

'Seek and ye shall find . . .'